BUS

ALLEN COUNTY PUBLIC

P9-EEC-368

this old dump

**Other books by Laura Jensen Walker**

*Girl Time*
*Thanks for the Mammogram!*
*Mentalpause*
*Dated Jekyll, Married Hyde*
*Love Handles for the Romantically Impaired*
*God Rest Ye Grumpy Scroogeymen,*
  with Michael Walker

# this old dump

## Renovate without Decking Your Mate

## LAURA JENSEN WALKER

Revell
Grand Rapids, Michigan

© 2004 by Laura Jensen Walker

Published by Fleming H. Revell
a division of Baker Publishing Group
P.O. Box 6287, Grand Rapids, MI 49516-6287
www.revellbooks.com

Printed in the United States of America

All rights reserved. No part of this publication may be reproduced, stored in a retrieval system, or transmitted in any form or by any means—for example, electronic, photocopy, recording—without the prior written permission of the publisher. The only exception is brief quotations in printed reviews.

Published in association with the literary agency of Alive Communications, Inc., 7680 Goddard Street, Suite 200, Colorado Springs, CO 80920.

Library of Congress Cataloging-in-Publication Data
Walker, Laura Jensen.
    This old dump : renovate without decking your mate / Laura Jensen Walker.
        p.    cm.
    ISBN 0-8007-5967-2 (pbk.)
    1. Dwellings—Maintenance and repair—Amateurs' manuals. 2. Dwellings—Remodeling—Amateurs' manuals.  I. Title.
TH4817.3.W35  2004
643′.7—dc22                                                         2004006779

Scripture is taken from the HOLY BIBLE, NEW INTERNATIONAL VERSION®. NIV®. Copyright © 1973, 1978, 1984 by International Bible Society. Used by permission of Zondervan. All rights reserved.

To Pat and Ken McLatchey,
cherished longtime friends and the king
and queen of home improvement

# contents

7

3 1833 04683 6266

# introduction

I n the classic 1950s film *All About Eve*, Bette Davis says
the memorable line "What a dump" as only Bette Davis
can.

I think she might have been talking about our house.
Seriously.

Buying a home is an exciting, albeit terrifying, experience.
Especially your first house. After stumbling glassy-eyed
into the twenty-seventh listing with your realtor, you begin
to learn that *cozy* means tiny and *charming* is just another
word for old.

But finally you've found, well, if not exactly your dream
home, at least one that won't give you nightmares.

Unless, of course, the remodeling takes ten years rather
than ten months and wipes out all your savings as well as
your kids' college fund.

There's nothing quite like the feeling when you first turn
the key in the lock and open the door to your brand-new
(at least to you), beautiful new home. Then you see the
ghastly flying-saucer light fixture from the sixties shining
down upon the grimy thirty-year-old, once beige carpet

and sneeze over the dusty once cream, now dark taupe living room drapes that come apart in your hands when you touch them.

As Dorothy said when she clicked those ruby red slippers together, "there's no place like home."

Easy enough for her to say. She never had to come up with a monthly mortgage payment.

Or lay carpet.

Or remodel a bathroom.

She just got to sing about bluebirds flying over the rainbow, run through a field of poppies, and get chased by some scary flying monkeys.

Trade ya, Dorothy.

Michael and I celebrated our happy home ownership milestone with a carpet picnic in the living room that first night. Actually, it was a one-of-his-colorful-quilts-on-the-dirty-old-carpet picnic. My beloved also presented me with a bouquet of flowers that graced the mantel of our charming, old-fashioned, formerly white, now dingy gray columned fireplace to mark the auspicious occasion.

But after the cheese and strawberries, Michael had to leave to rehearse for a play he was performing in.

I smiled, kissed my husband good-bye, and encouraged him to "break a leg." And the moment he walked out the door, my itching fingers started yanking up that dirty, ugly carpet to reveal the gleaming hardwood floors beneath, which I'd discovered during our walk-through.

That was just the beginning of an ongoing renovation that continues to this day.

Although our house was considered a "cosmetic" fixer-upper—the original owner even knocked ten thousand dollars off the asking price for that very reason—we had no clue how much makeup it would take to make it even remotely presentable.

And we're still powdering our house's nose to this day.

Within these pages you'll discover the joys, frustrations, and utter chaos of remodeling, redecorating, and maintaining a home. Think *The Money Pit* meets *Trading Spaces*. Whether you've just bought your first house or have already been there and done that construction dance down the home-improvement hardwood floor for years and years, I hope you'll enjoy these funny fixer-upper tales—and maybe even learn a thing or two.

Like how to renovate your home without decking your mate.

---

*A little house—a house of my own—out of the wind's and the rain's way.*

---

—PADRAIC COLUM

# 1

# home not-so-sweet home improvement

• • •

*Ah, for those carefree, halcyon days when we were happy-go-lucky renters without a maintenance care in the world.*

I used to think fixing something meant picking up the phone and saying, 'Hello, maintenance?'" my girlfriend Katie said, "but now I'm the one on the other end of the phone."

Katie was the ultimate city girl—the Windy City. Born and bred in the toddlin' town of Chicago, in her early twenties she moved to Sacramento, California, where she happily rented an apartment for many years.

Then she met, fell in love with, and married Mark, the six-foot-two wine-country boy in shining armor who lived in the beautiful Sonoma Valley of California.

Can you say *Green Acres*?

Katie had just a teeny-tiny bit of difficulty adjusting at first. Oh, not to the beauty of her surroundings. Not at all. When she sat at her dining room table with her morning cup of coffee and looked out at their two and one-third acres of rich green pasture and rolling hills, she was blessed beyond belief at the to-die-for view in her "new" forty-year-old ranch-style home.

It was just the whole living in the country bit that my city-girl friend had trouble adapting to. The dust, the distance from town, and the animals—she quickly learned to feed goats, horses, sheep, rabbits, dogs, and cats. Not to mention two children.

Katie, who's always been a whiz with numbers, handled the finances in her new ready-made family but couldn't quite figure out what her groom meant when he kept asking her, "Do you have something set aside for house maintenance?"

Then the water heater broke, and they didn't have the few hundred dollars to fix it.

"How was I supposed to know you're supposed to budget for that?" my friend asked.

Even housekeeping was a shock to Katie. No matter how much she cleaned, there was that dirt-road country dust thing to contend with. Every maintenance issue, every project, boggled my city-girl friend's mind. "I knew how to do nothing," Katie said. She also quickly learned that nothing's cheap in the country. "By the time someone comes out here, they charge you just for driving out all this way."

Recently, what started out as a simple repair job in one of their bathrooms—because it's an older home and they live close to the beach, they had termite damage under the bathroom—turned into a remodel of both baths.

"My ignorance knows no bounds in these areas," Katie said. "I went out to price what the bathrooms were going to cost and underestimated by about half. I'm good with numbers, so my husband trusted me implicitly." My math-whiz friend generally estimates that any home-improvement project will cost about 25 percent more than she plans and, for some obscure reason, will always need to have an electrician.

But the whole bathroom remodel thing was uncharted territory for Katie.

"I went from understanding that fixtures don't come with the shower to knowing you can special order a toilet paper holder," she said. (Which she did, by the way.)

> My math-whiz friend generally estimates that any home-improvement project will cost about 25 percent more than she plans and, for some obscure reason, will always need to have an electrician.

When they went to retrofit the shower in the master bath—for which she had already ordered special glass for the door—Katie's brother-in-law, who's a glazier, had to give them the bad news that due to space constraints, it couldn't be retrofitted. He recommended tearing down the privacy half wall that separated the toilet from the rest of the bath and installing a new corner shower instead.

"Now that I understand walls can be taken down without much effort, my husband's really in trouble," Katie said.

My friend also bought a four-hundred-dollar toilet for the new bathroom just because she liked the look of it. "I should never have gone into the hardware store," Katie said ruefully, adding that once she bought the one, she had to get another for the other bath that was also being remodeled. She also chose brushed steel fixtures with a bit of gold trim. "I went out to get the faucets and showerheads one day, and that stuff alone was seven hundred dollars!" she said incredulously. "I couldn't believe the price of stuff!"

> **"Your house always knows when you have an extra dime," Katie said. "Something always breaks."**

The sticker shock was all the more pronounced for Katie and Mark, who always pay as they go for any project, both of them unwilling to get caught up in the whole home equity loan game.

"Your house always knows when you have an extra dime," Katie said. "Something always breaks. When you're in the country, there's a myriad of things that can go wrong, from a well needing a new pump to things like septic tanks. Who knew?"

My friend Maria and her husband, Ralph, ran into that same country-living rude awakening.

When they moved from Sacramento, California, to Pukwana, South Dakota, five miles north of a city of 380 people and ten miles away from the big city of Chamberlain (population 2,500), they soon learned that they were not going to have any help fixing and renovating the 1920s farmhouse they'd just bought.

Before relocating in a hurry, the young couple who owned the house prior to Ralph and Maria had started to do some major home improvements. The house had been jacked up so that a fresh basement could be poured, it had new plumbing and wiring and fresh Sheetrock that had been plastered, and it had new kitchen cabinets and fixtures—"Everything!" Maria said, "except that the only door that was hanging was in the bathroom, and none of the beautiful oak baseboards or window and door trims were up. They were still in the basement, marked on the back as to where they went.

"Guess what it's like coming in the house without baseboards, etc.?" my friend asked. "Field mice and flies. Long story short, we city slickers tried to hire someone to do it for us. We had a member of one contracting company come out to look at the mess. Imagine eighty years worth of paint on baseboards we wanted stripped for the 'beautiful oak.' Also think of what we didn't think of at the time—it was all marked according to someone else's scheme of things. We hadn't a clue what went where."

And the house was built at a time when nothing was standard.

"We were told they'd get back to us with an estimate in two weeks," Maria recalled. She waited and called after two weeks and was told they were busy and it would take another two weeks. Pretty soon Ralph and Maria realized that "two weeks" meant "I'd rather not accept this job."

"Inspired by a romantic notion of do-it-yourself projects, we gave each other his 'n' her nail belts for Christmas, along with a *Reader's Digest* guide to building," she said.

19

That was the beginning of a six-year home-improvement project.

The first thing the transplanted city slickers did was try to put up a door. "All we had to do was find it," Maria recalled. "These were heavy, solid oak doors with the hardware still on them. *Good*, we thought." Except the couple also had to find the frame for the door, which wasn't on the house, nor by the door. "The project was like putting together the pieces of a puzzle," she said. "We had to find the right combination of door and frame, which took us to an old chicken coop out back in addition to the basement. I don't like things that go bump in the night and was frightened of all the garden snakes that popped up there, so hauling jambs and doors to see what fit where while at the same time keeping an eye out for snakes made me feel I was playing *Green Acres* with Ralph."

Maria recalls one day in particular when they were going into town—Chamberlain—for a social meeting with some members of the hospital board. (Ralph's a surgeon.) "I was so tired and beside myself from all the work that when asked what I'd have to drink, I said, 'Give me a Long Island iced tea' when everyone else was having soda," she said. "It was an interesting moment, because I don't drink that much and when I do have the occasional drink, it's usually wine.

"Everyone in the room stopped to listen because I probably sounded like someone desperate for booze."

At that point, Maria was too tired to care. Then the pregnant wife of a board member came over, put her arm around Maria, and said, "Honey, I know just what you mean. I'd have one with you if I weren't pregnant."

The two women became instant friends that day.

By the third year, the couple had the hang of it. "It was actually fun for me to go to a store like Home Depot when we visited Kansas City," Maria said. "I particularly loved impressing the salespeople with my newfound wisdom about leveling, beveling, and planing with straight edges or water tubes."

As husband and wife gained confidence in their abilities, they started doing some things around the house "from scratch." Maria said, "We put in concrete slabs and built porches—with roofs that would stand up to the Dakota winters."

The hardest part of leaving their house six years later for a new job location was working on it until the last minute. "We were still stripping floors and putting up ceiling trim until the very end," Maria recalled. "Unfortunately, since the previous owners had done such a good job putting in new flooring, walls, etc., none of the trim fit. The wood they used back in those days (the '20s) was full-measure wood: A two-by-four was actually two whole inches by four whole inches. Today it's more like $1^3/_4$ by $3^1/_2$, which made learning a bit harder for us in the beginning."

Yet doing those years of home-improvement work on their lovely South Dakota farmhouse also helped when they had to move and buy a bargain home in Kansas City. "When we looked with a realtor, the house needed some real work, as the linoleum was coming up off the kitchen floor, there was a half-finished basement, and all the carpet had stinky pet stains on it," Maria said. "We bought it knowing we could pull up the carpet and install tile flooring ourselves."

The couple also rented some heavy equipment to allow them to lift an indoor hot tub up from the basement so they could stop the wood rot. Then they tore out and reinstalled fresh lumber where the wood had rotted—a fairly big job. "We knew we could do it, and we did," Maria said proudly.

"And as a result, we got a great house for a good price in the bargain."

I'm impressed! So, Maria, do you and Ralph want to come back to Sacramento for a visit, say sometime next spring, when at long last we'll tackle our kitchen remodel? Just don't forget your his 'n' her nail belts.

When my friends Jan and Carl got married nearly a decade ago, they opted to keep and remodel her house and sell his. "We can do all the work ourselves," Carl suggested, telling Jan *again* how he'd spent ten years renovating a Victorian where he'd learned a lot. "It'll be fun."

So immediately after the honeymoon, they rolled up their sleeves and went to work on his Sacramento duplex. "We painted and tore up the landscaping, mostly," Jan recalled. "It was heaven working alongside my husband, shades of the past, when as a young married woman with my first man, we spent hours together building our nest."

After Carl and Jan sold the duplex, they tackled the cabin they'd hastily decided to buy right before the wedding. "It was a steal because it was mostly uninhabited for twenty years—at least by humans," Jan recalled. "Armies of mice had made it their command center." And the original shake-shingled roof, circa 1947, leaked everywhere. "It was built by a farmer after World War II with scrap wood from his barn—probably never meant to last fifty years. The wood framing on the backside of the cabin was badly rotted and sagging tremendously. Plus, the twenty-one-member cabin owners' association had drilled three dry wells and spent twenty thousand dollars trying to get potable water. For decades, the water source was a secret creek up the hill that happily flowed into old oak storage tanks dotted with woodpecker holes. Most cabin owners brought up bottled water," Jan said. "No big deal. Nobody ever died from brushing their teeth, but the county threatened to shut down the cabins if they didn't produce water without little microscopic bugs in it."

Hurray for the obstacles. The sale price got cheaper with every problem.

They just "had" to buy this place set amidst towering pines at six thousand feet, away from the often-unbearable summer heat of the Sacramento Valley. "We've discovered we're suckers for potential," Jan said. "The fact that the U.S. Forest Service owns the ground it sits on and we had to pay to lease this land from them, renewable every twenty years if they so choose, never deterred us. We would restore it and a piece of history at the same time."

Mountain Utopia, here they come.

They soon discovered, however, that the Forest Service had file cabinets of regulations about cabin restoration. Inside you could do what you pleased, but nothing on the outside could be altered from the original design, and all had to be approved. The government required owners to repair things on the structure "in kind." Which meant no new windows unless they looked exactly like the originals, and new wood sash double-hung windows were out of the question on their budget. The doors had to look like the ones that came off. The problem: The front and back doors were just pieces of old plywood hinged without frames, with three-inch gaps where the mouse armies came and went.

"How can we recreate these?" they inquired of the Forest Service.

"Just make sure the new doors have the exact same design," they were told.

"Saw blade grooves were a design? Okay, so we'll comply," Jan said. How hard could it be to buy some doors and frame them, after all? "Ha! The old farmer hadn't known about Home Depot and how stock doors only come in a few sizes. To frame stock doors meant we'd have to literally tear down the walls and start over." The couple finally found a contractor who said he could get nice birch solid core doors to fit for around two hundred dollars each.

*Yikes*, they thought. And he'd have no idea until he started the job how much labor it would be. "We agreed, gave him the key, and went home," Jan recalled. "By the time it was done, we'd spent fifteen hundred dollars."

No two doors have ever been more admired. "Come on in," Jan will say when you arrive at her cabin. "Now aren't these the most beautiful doors you've ever seen?"

Some of their projects are buried, however. In the early days when the toilet clogged up repeatedly, Carl mentioned it to a cabin neighbor who said, "It's typical in the forest. Tree roots strangle the leach lines." So Carl started digging. Yep, tree roots, so he phoned Roto-Rooter, and they "brought one of their thingies out to grind out the problems." Oops.

"Hey, you've got no leach lines here," Mr. Roto-Rooter told them.

In the midst of this story, I had to reveal my rural ignorance to Jan. "Um, what's a leach line exactly?"

"Oh, it's a perforated pipe, like a long sieve, attached to your septic tank," my country friend answered with a smirk. "Shall I explain how it works—or in this case, didn't?"

I passed. Ignorance is bliss when it comes to flushing toilets—city or country.

"So we made a run to the Twain Harte hardware store twenty miles away and bought the plastic pipe," Jan continued. "Carl handed me a pickax and gave instructions. Suddenly, in dirt up over my ankles, digging pipe line to carry sewage, working with my husband wasn't so romantic anymore."

Then there was the day they hauled all the old furniture out of the cabin, especially the mattresses that housed generations of mouse families. "We even found a family of mice nested very dead in the vacuum cleaner," Jan said. "Suddenly the cheap price of the cabin didn't seem like such a steal after all. We were definitely paying our dues."

And then some, I'd say. The couple has lovingly upgraded Bumblebee Summer Home Tract, much to the delight of their cabin neighbors.

Kudos to you, Jan. And, Carl, I hope you appreciate your darling little rugged country girl who has such strong pioneer stock flowing through her veins. Michael knows that my veins would have collapsed under the mouse assault and my screams would have brought the cabin walls tumbling down like Jericho.

Jeannie and Johnny, some friends of ours who pastor a church in California, also had some rodent visitors for a while in their newly purchased 1880 Queen Anne Victorian. "Rats were our house guests for about two years," Johnny recalled. "Especially over our bed at night, we could hear them chewing in the attic. I'd bang on the ceiling, and it would scare them for a little while." Once the scaffolding was put in place to paint the exterior, he could trim the trees hanging over the house (these were tree rats that would jump from the branches onto the roof and make their way inside the house through a hole in the attic). "Until then, I was emptying an attic trap every day," he said. "Rats are really ugly."

I couldn't agree more, Johnny. I'm absolutely terrified of rats.

When we first moved into our fifty-year-old house, Michael and I were out in the still mostly empty garage, where he was poking through old cupboards while I sat and chatted with him on the bottom step of the two-step staircase into the garage. Suddenly a rat—which looked gigantic to me but Michael insists was small, or perhaps even just a large mouse (I don't *think* so, honey!)—disturbed by all the noise, came streaking across the floor at my feet.

I let out a bloodcurdling scream and immediately lifted up my shaking legs. Thankfully, Michael was there to rescue me and went to the local hardware store, where he immediately bought some rat traps—which naturally snapped in the middle of the night so my poor husband had to get up and dispose of them while I stayed in bed quaking beneath the covers with my legs drawn up to my chest.

When Jeannie and Johnny first moved into their three-story, 3900-square-foot, more-than-a-century-old Victorian downtown, it was a duplex and they couldn't get from their bedroom to the kitchen without going outside—which definitely limited late-night snacking in bed.

The couple really had their renovation work cut out for them.

Their kitchen alone took a year to remodel, and Jeannie said she served hundreds of people that year with no cabinets. They saved only one tiny counter hooked to the original six-inch deep kitchen sink through that year of remodeling. All their food, pots and pans, etc., were in boxes on the floor of the dining room that whole time.

"It was like camping," Jeannie recalled. "We used a lot of paper plates, plastic cups, and plastic silverware."

"People loved to visit us and see the rebuilding process and progress from their last visit," she said. The large kitchen, now a breathtaking vision with its soft buttercream cabinets, black granite countertops, reproduction light fixtures, complementary buttercream tile floor, and striking black wallpaper with rosy-pink apples and grapes with touches of buttercream, topped off by crown molding, has now been completed for more than two years, and the couple still hears stories of how fun it was to watch the process. "I always smile inside when people talk about the fun of watching a remodel," Jeannie said. "Were they here 24/7? Did they have to live with the dirt, dust, and depression?"

It was all worth it though. Both Johnny and Jeannie love their gorgeous, to-die-for kitchen (which I'm not lusting over in the least . . . really!). They proudly showed me the original floor-to-ceiling red-brick cooking area they uncovered under decades of lath and plaster. The couple decided to blend the old and the new by exposing the long-hidden brick chimney and paying homage to the beauty of the original construction.

In the summer and fall of 2002, my cousin Barb and her husband, Frank, were adding a "simple addition" to their late-nineteenth-century rural Wisconsin farmhouse. They needed to add a bathroom off the rear entrance, a sewing room for Barb, and a coat closet.

Not too difficult, they thought.

So they got estimates that ranged from twenty-five thousand to thirty thousand dollars and budgeted for them. Then the work began.

"The first thing that happened," Barb recalled, "was they started digging the hole for the basement and foundations. As the excavator was digging away, first he hit the electric line that ran from the well to the house. Then he was digging some more, when all of a sudden we heard everyone yelling—in Spanish, of course, because no one spoke English. They were all running around and jumping into the hole."

The couple ran outside and discovered a gaping hole under the entire southeast corner of the house where the footing had collapsed. The house was built in 1870, and the only footings they used in those days were piles of rocks—about three feet high. Their basement was made out of big boulders and was only five feet, six inches high. "It had held the house up all these years, until we disturbed the rocks," Barb said.

Now what were they supposed to do?

Their builder decided that they needed to pour a ten-foot by thirty-foot cement wall right next to the old wall for support. "We could just see the dollar signs ka-chinging up," Barb recalled.

Then the inspector came and checked everything out. He decided that since they were adding another bathroom, they now had to bring both their water and old septic tank system up to code.

That's when they hired a contractor.

"Big mistake," Barb said.

Now they had to move their well fifteen feet farther away from the house, bring all the controls inside the foundation, update the septic tank, and install a whole new wash bed. "Everything had to be redone and put farther away from the house," my cousin recalled. "Ka-ching, ka-ching, another thirty thousand dollars in one fell swoop. We'd already doubled our budget and weren't even out of the ground.

"It was one headache after another," Barb said. "I tried to avoid my husband as much as possible during the construction, because he was walking a tightrope with the contractors and getting pretty snarly."

One day, nearing the completion of the remodel when the carpenters were still madly working away, my cousin needed to go upstairs to their bedroom and pack a suitcase for a trip she was leaving for that afternoon. "I was throwing things in the suitcase, when Mother Nature spoke to me," Barb recalled. "I walked into our L-shaped bathroom, sat down on the stool in a hurry (at my age you can't hold it), then looked up, and lo and behold, the carpenter was standing in the window frame, trying to insert the new window, and he had the biggest grin on his face.

"I started panicking—*How do I get out of here?*" my cousin remembered. She had jeans and an oversized sweatshirt on, so she figured she'd just pull her shirt down over her knees and back out the door. "Once out the door," Barb said, "I pulled my pants up, my shirt down, and turned around to finish packing. Then I looked up, and there in the other window was another carpenter with a big grin on his face. He saw it all and thought I was mooning him! My face turned beet red, and I was sure glad to be leaving that afternoon."

Gee, cousin, I think that gives new meaning to worker's compensation.

---

*The physician can bury his mistakes, but the architect can only advise his client to plant vines.*

—FRANK LLOYD WRIGHT

# 2

# what happens when your cosmetic fixer-upper needs a lot of makeup

...

*The foundation was fine, but the harvest-gold linoleum, screaming orange-floral wallpaper, and chocolate-brown sink made me blush.*

**M**ichael and I had been married just over three years and living in a series of rentals—apartments, duplexes, and houses—when I got the craving for a home of our own. One where we could choose our own carpets and wall colors, plant what we liked in the backyard, and hammer as many nail holes into the walls as we wanted.

My sweetheart was a trifle hesitant at first about taking such a big step.

When we were dating, we were both rather free-spirited and carefree and open to living wherever the wind blew us. I'd lived in Europe for five years in my early twenties, and Michael had traveled all over the world in his entertainment job on a cruise ship, so we were both open to the possibility of living overseas somewhere together one day—for a season or two. If not overseas, then maybe the Oregon or Washington coast. Or perhaps Vermont, with its yummy maple syrup, sleigh rides, and Norman Rockwell small-town life. (Although we quickly scratched the latter, knowing my California native boy couldn't handle the harsh winters.)

My honey was a little reluctant to plunge into the world of home ownership. He kept repeating that old saying, "You don't own a house; the house owns you." But after seeing we owed the IRS again, he saw the tax write-off wisdom of the move. So we found a realtor and began looking.

We briefly considered buying our starter home in one of the many hot new developments popping up all over Sacramento and its outlying suburbs.

At least I did.

There was something tremendously appealing about beginning our homeowner lives with a shiny, pristine slate and choosing our own floor coverings, cupboards, countertops, and fixtures. And myriad fun upgrades.

But my sweetheart, who has the ultimate green thumb and a penchant for growing things, couldn't warm to the idea of tiny lots and postage-stamp backyards with nothing but dirt.

And no full-grown trees anywhere.

Michael has a love affair with trees. Nice leafy, mature trees that have stood the test of time. Not little saplings all in a row in identical front yards up and down the street.

Which is why we decided to look for an older home in a well-established neighborhood filled with trees. Thankfully, Sacramento is called "the city of trees," so there were plenty of green neighborhoods to choose from. Unfortunately, the ones with the century-old Victorians or charming brick cottages that I fell in love with were just a little out of our price range.

Can you say triple our budget?

Plus, since Michael worked thirty minutes east of Sacramento and at the time I commuted forty-five minutes south, we needed a central location between the two workplaces. That's why we finally narrowed our search to one quiet, older area with some lovely outlying neighborhoods lush with trees and greenery yet with close enough access to the freeway.

Now the hunt was on.

Like all first-time homeowners, we had visions of *House Beautiful* and *Better Homes and Gardens* in our heads. All at a reasonable price, of course. And in turnkey condition. We wanted it all, but we soon realized that wasn't an option.

> **Like all first-time homeowners, we had visions of *House Beautiful* and *Better Homes and Gardens* in our heads.**

There were a few things, however, that weren't negotiable.

Michael had to have a two-car garage.

I had to have a two-bath, or at least two-toilet, home.

We both agreed on three bedrooms—one for us, one for an office, and one for a craft room/guest room.

32

We looked.

And looked.

And looked.

But nothing was ever quite right. Sometimes we found three bedrooms but only one bath. Other times we found two baths and three bedrooms but only a one-car garage. Once or twice we found all the items on our list, but the houses were in such appalling condition that it would have cost all four arms and four legs between us just to make them livable.

At last we found a darling little thousand-square-foot cottage on a quiet, tree-lined street with original hardwood floors and the cutest kitchen I'd ever seen—my dream kitchen, in fact.

I was sold.

Done up in blue and white, the kitchen looked like something from a home decorating magazine, with its sparkling navy-and-white checkerboard floor, snowy bead-board cabinets, gleaming white updated appliances, and built-in white corner cupboards displaying *my* Blue Willow china.

It was a sign.

"This is it, honey. This is the house I want."

Michael exchanged a glance with Brian, the realtor. "Sweetie, it's only two bedrooms."

"Well, there are only two of us," I replied in my glassy-eyed dream-kitchen trance. "We could make do with two bedrooms."

"But, honey," my husband pointed out practically, "it's only a one-car garage."

"So? Couldn't we park one of the cars in the driveway instead?" I asked, salivating over the adorable corner cupboards in my advanced state of kitchen envy.

"But, darling, there's only one small bathroom."

I let out a heavy sigh of small-bladder regret as I tore my lusting eyes away. "All right. But that's how I want *our* kitchen to look."

"Understood."

Brian trooped us through a succession of several more homes to no avail. Who knew it would be so difficult to find a simple three-bedroom, two-bath house with a two-car garage? The problem was that although that was the minimum standard in new homes from the late 1970s on, in the area where we were house hunting, most of the homes had been built in the 1950s.

And the standard then was generally two bedrooms, one bath, and a one-car garage. It was a luxury to have three bedrooms and a two-car garage. And two baths as well? Unheard of, unless the homeowner had remodeled.

At long last, however, and much to our tired realtor's relief, we found a three bedroom, one-and-a-half bath (which worked for me, since it was the two toilets I really wanted), two-car garage home with the added bonus of a small den and fabulous hardwood floors.

More than anything, however, what sold us on the house was the yard.

The front yard had a gorgeous fifty-year-old Modesto ash tree that provided ample shade, but it was the rear of the house that was a real revelation. The three sides of the backyard were ringed with a canopy of trees and decades-old ivy that provided a romantic cocoon of shade and privacy. We couldn't even *see* our neighbors' homes through the trees, and vice versa.

As a still relatively new married couple in that honeymoon stage, it worked for us. We felt as if we were on our own private domestic island.

Sold!

The only problem: Our cozy little fifty-year-old ranch-style cottage was what you'd call a "cosmetic fixer-upper." Which is just another way of saying ugly and outdated.

And nowhere was this more evident than in the kitchen from the sixties netherworld.

This 10 x 11 square of hideousness was as far away from my blue-and-white dream kitchen as Greenland is from sun-drenched

> **Our cozy little fifty-year-old ranch-style cottage was what you'd call a "cosmetic fixer-upper." Which is just another way of saying ugly and outdated.**

Hawaii. Dog-food-tan cupboards, yellowish-gold walls, not-quite-avocado-more-like-pistachio-green tile countertops with gray trim, a shallow diarrhea-brown sink without a garbage disposal, and sickly harvest-gold linoleum that looked like the aftermath of a rock concert.

Worst of all was the orange-and-yellow daisy wallpaper with specks of lime green covering one wall.

My skin started to itch, and I began to shudder and twitch in bad-taste convulsions.

But Brian, our realtor, who had bought and fixed up several homes of his own over the years, came to the rescue with a resuscitating shot of renovating reassurance. "A little paint, a little paper, some new flooring and countertops, and you can easily turn this into the kitchen of your dreams."

Relieved, I told Michael, who was head-over-heels about the yard, "Okay, but before we move in, we *have* to remodel the kitchen. There's no way I could cook in there without getting sick!"

Nearly nine years later, I've cooked a zillion meals in the still-not-remodeled kitchen and have only gotten sick a few times.

Sure, we've made several cosmetic improvements—painting all the walls and cupboards white, ripping off the orange-and-yellow daisy wallpaper and replacing it with a subtle white-and-blue patterned paper, removing the dog-food-colored upper cabinet doors that no longer shut due to years and layers of accumulated paint, replacing the ancient leaky faucet with a gleaming-chrome gooseneck one, and installing a new white stove and refrigerator. My artistic husband also stenciled a cute blue-and-white teacup border above the window and sewed some pretty blue-and-white china patterned curtains with eyelet trim (yep, he's the one in the family who's handy with a needle, not me). And I, the decorating queen, took several of my Blue Willow plates, along with some of our favorite blue-and-white Staffordshire ones we'd collected on visits to England, and arranged them in a beautiful semicircle on the white-with-tiny-blue-diamonds wallpaper.

The plates make a dramatic focal point and help draw the eye up from the pistachio-and-gray countertops, chocolate-brown sink, and still-harvest-gold floor.

I was more than a little clueless about kitchen remodeling costs.

In fact, when I first received the contract to write this book, I thought we could use the advance money to pay for my long-awaited kitchen makeover—which I could then detail at length here for you, my reader. Instead, the check went to a broken air conditioner, some unexpected car repairs, and sundry bills.

Don't you hate bills?

Fortunately, my publisher decided to hold off on the publication date for another year because they wanted me to write another book first.

Fine by me. By then we would definitely have enough money saved to do the kitchen remodel, which I could joyously recount here.

Not quite.

Other unexpected expenses arose, including a vacation to England, which my work-stressed husband desperately needed. It was quite a sacrifice to return to the land of storybook cottages, milky tea, and ancient cathedrals, but one I lovingly made for my beloved.

Thankfully, my publisher rode to the rescue a second time. Once again they delayed publication of *This Old Dump* for me to write another book instead. Whew. Another several months' reprieve. Certainly before my new deadline we'd have ample money set aside to at long last tackle our kitchen renovation so I could write about it for you here.

And if not, we could always take out a home equity loan to finance the project *and* pay off existing bills. Right?

Wrong. And I knew it. Years of reading Mary Hunt's *Cheapskate Monthly* newsletter had taught me that taking out a home equity loan—especially when you're already in consumer debt—would not be the smartest move.

In fact, in her newest book, *Debt-Proof Your Marriage* (Revell, 2003), which I highly recommend, Mary says, "A home equity loan (appropriately referred to in the industry as HEL) is a second mortgage secured by the equity on your home. The nature of a HEL makes it risky because it can easily turn stupid. If you borrow against your equity to clean up your credit card debt and then run up your credit cards all over again, that leaves you with twice the debt—the

HEL and the credit cards. It is not intelligent to use an appreciating asset (home equity) to pay for depreciating goods and services (credit card balances)" (107–8).

Okay, Mary. Got it. I was only tempted for an hour . . . um, week or two.

Consequently, we still don't have our remodeled kitchen. Today as I type this on my office laptop, the hideous harvest-gold flooring, avocado-pistachio countertops, and *no* dishwasher still wink at me mockingly.

I finally realized that the only way I'm ever going to get my kitchen renovated is for this book to sell beaucoup copies so I can get a nice fat royalty check.

And you can help me out, if you would, please. If you'd like to have a part in making my long-dreamed-for kitchen remodel come true, please spread the word and tell all your friends to buy a copy of this book. (And once that big royalty check arrives and the kitchen is finished, I promise to post pictures on my website, www.laurajensenwalker.com, so you can see the results of your domestic assistance. Thanks so much!)

The kitchen wasn't the only part of the house that needed a little cosmetic touch-up.

The previous owners had erected a non-load-bearing wall inside the den so as to create a narrow, claustrophobic hallway (think a bowling alley lane for hobbits) to access the back bedroom and half bath add-on. We could barely walk through it without hyperventilating. Once, after one too many breakfast pastries, my hips nearly got wedged between the two walls!

So with the professional help of my contractor brother, Dave, knocking down that non-load-bearing wall was one of the first things we did. (There's nothing like swinging a sledgehammer to make a woman feel strong and powerful.

Try it sometime.) After Sheetrocking over one of the now two doors to the den, it was time to texture—another first for us.

It wasn't until years later when we were talking to a home-remodeling guru and asked, "How come our texture is so rough and pointy?" that we learned that after you blow the texture on with the texture-gun thingamabob, you're supposed to come behind and smooth it out with a trowel-dealy.

Oops. Oh well, I've only scraped my knuckles on the wall a couple times. We've got plenty of Band-Aids.

Removing the grubby tan carpet in the living room and dining room was another noteworthy experience for the cosmetic home-improvement history books. It took us weeks and weeks to painstakingly remove the hundreds of staples in the original hardwood floor—spaced every two inches apart—that had held the carpet padding in place. (The pad was so old that when we pulled it up, it disintegrated into piles of sand. Not exactly a day at the beach.)

But it was a walk in the park compared to our friend Shane's house.

Our single friend, who attends our weekly Bible study, recently bought his first house—a charming two-bedroom, one-bath 1938 art deco style home with wonderful architectural detailing in an older, established part of town. Shane's place was also called a "cosmetic fixer-upper" because nothing was *structurally* wrong with the house.

However, a sixties remodel had left everything "pretty hideous," he said.

Although the kitchen had nice oak cabinets, the linoleum and wallpaper were a mixture of golds, greens, and browns—"a stew of corn and peas," Shane said. Plus, sometime in the seventies, a previous owner did away with any kind of ventilation in the kitchen, so when Shane moved in some thirty years later, there was a fine layer of grease everywhere.

Shane, who is quite an artistic individual with a minimalist, contemporary style—those *Trading Spaces* designers have nothing on him—had lots to do to tailor his new home to his taste. For some reason, he wasn't crazy about the "pretty little grandma stencils of flowers" in the living room, the "cutesy sea foam green walls" in the bath, the French Country front door, or the Victorian six-panel doors and door casings in the hall, dining room, and bath, which he says didn't "jive in the least with the house's deco bones."

"I now know exactly what people mean by 'a house with good bones,'" Shane said. "My home's bones reflect a hodgepodge of eras, decorating whims, and just plain bad taste—ceiling fans with those little frosted glass shades that take you right back to Grandma's house, green sheet linoleum floors with faux marble flecks, and mirrored ceilings in the bath."

Additionally, the bathroom cabinets under the sink vanity were a dark brown laminate that someone had painted white—and in many places left large pieces of the blue painter's tape—and linoleum was peeling away from the walls here and there throughout the house.

The back bedroom, which Shane planned to use as his, had mold stains on the walls. "Evidently, the windows weren't closing well," he said. "The former owners didn't do anything except put posters over the mold, or furniture against it. They had buried the place in so much junk, they didn't even realize what was there. If only those walls could talk . . . They looked like they had a hundred miles of bad road on them."

There were also old steel grid windows in the living room and bedroom that had rust all over them. "I didn't notice until after I moved in that some of the painting on the wall was a little 'bubbly,'" Shane recalled. "There was a rainstorm the first week after I moved in, and it sounded like someone was lightly pouring water onto the floor."

It turns out it was coming in through the windows. Shane was concerned because he thought it would be a costly problem to fix, but once he cleaned out the gutters, it stopped. Apparently, the previous owners never cleaned the gutters. This was only the beginning of the saga of Shane's major remodeling project. (To find out the rest of the story, read chapter 7, "The Worker Waltz.")

At least my friend now has a drop-dead gorgeous remodeled kitchen with granite countertops. But I'm not bitter. Not at all.

---

*I want a house that has got over all its troubles;*
*I don't want to spend the rest of my life bringing up*
*a young and inexperienced house.*

---

—JEROME K. JEROME

# 3

# paint to the left, paint to the right, stand up, sit down, fight fight fight! (or, his 'n' her painting styles)

...

*He says two coats; I say one. He says up and down; I say round and round.*

Painting's all about personality. And that other *P* word: perfection.

Who's the perfectionist in your home? Him or her? I have to confess that in our household, my husband is—in most areas (although the picking-up-after-himself bit somehow fell through the perfectionist cracks, as did the picture and knickknack angling—that's where I come in). But he's most definitely Mr. Take-his-time-everything-has-to-be-perfect when it comes to painting.

As I quickly learned the first time we painted together. Not a pretty picture.

First, I didn't pour the paint out of the can the proper way. Then my brush strokes weren't going the right direction. Then he wanted me to use different brushes for different areas. Then he thought I was just a little too fast with the roller. (The pinpoints of paint turning my hair an early white gave me away.)

> **But what really set my perfectionist painter husband's brush strokes on edge was when he realized I hadn't taken the time to mask everything off.**

But what really set my perfectionist painter husband's brush strokes on edge was when he realized I hadn't taken the time to mask everything off.

"Honey, where's the masking tape?"

I pointed across the room with my left hand while I kept painting with my right. "Over there."

"No, I mean, where's the masking tape around the window and countertops to protect them?"

I snorted. "These countertops don't need protecting. Wouldn't bother me a bit if they turned white. And we can use a razor blade on the window. Besides, masking takes too much time."

Our friend Mike Duncan agrees. "Painting is the reward," he says. "It's the prep work that'll kill you."

Carl is cut from the same painter's cloth as Michael. His wife, Jan, my country girl pal whom you met in chapter 1, calls him "Mr. Organized."

"Though I'd been a single homeowner for twelve years and managed just fine, he insisted on teaching me how to paint 'properly,'" Jan recalled. "He showed me how to pour the paint into small buckets so I don't slop it from the gallon, which had always worked for me. He showed me how to clean the brushes each time (Excuse me? I'm painting again in two hours!) until I showed him an episode of *Room by Room* on the Home and Garden channel and the handy hint about just wrapping up your paintbrush in a Ziploc bag and storing it in the fridge until next time—it stays perfectly fresh with the paint on."

Carl told his sweetheart, "Jan, these are expensive brushes. They must be properly cleaned."

"Well, then buy me the cheap ones," Jan said. "I'm a use-it-and-toss-it kind of gal."

Her husband tried to explain that the cheap ones "shed" like their cat. "You don't want hairs coming off, do you?"

"Do you really want to know?" she asked. "Who cares? Nobody will notice a few hairs here and there."

Jan admits that she gets more paint on her than on the wall. "One day while we were painting a kitchen in one of our rental houses (We're suckers for potential, remember? Always fixing up houses and getting so attached we can't sell them), I had the gallon of paint up on the countertop—not a little bit in a small plastic bucket as Carl had instructed earlier—and stepped down right into it," she confessed. Luckily, Carl was away at the hardware store, so she quickly sopped it up so he wouldn't notice.

"How come so much paint is missing from this can?" he asked upon his return.

Jan just shrugged.

The summer after the couple first got married, they painted their little cabin in the woods, and Carl, "the perfectionist," made Jan scrape every layer of flaky paint off, down to the bare wood. "Then we 'permanized' it by painting on this elastomeric stuff that expands and contracts with the weather," Jan recalled. "Carl swears by it, as it worked so well on his Victorian. Weeks later we got to paint. All the cabin neighbors came by to check it out, as we had the ugliest cabin in the twenty-one-cabin development and they were applauding our work. We finally set up chairs in the front so they could have paint-side seats."

Jan admits, however, that the paint has lasted for eight years because Carl is so thorough. "Me, I'm a close-enough-is-good-enough, slap-it-up-there kind of gal," she said.

That's why we're friends.

In that regard, Jan and I are exactly the same in most of the home-improvement areas of our lives: "Close enough is good enough."

Over the years, "Carl the Meticulous" has learned to laugh at his less-than-meticulous wife. "Not so much in the beginning," Jan said, "but I came with a manufacturer's warning: Works fast and messy."

My friends always have issues over paint colors. Since Jan can never choose from a microscopic paint chip, they buy quarts of paint and have stripes painted on every wall until they get the right shade. "Too much pink," she says. So Carl runs down to their local paint store and has them mix another color. After at least five tries, they both finally give up and choose one. Jan said, "I always say, 'Not quite right, but I guess we'll have to live with it.' Then two weeks later, I never notice."

What I want to know is what's up with those paint chip sheets? We spend hours agonizing over just the exact shade we want, then we go buy the paint, and when we brush it on, it never ever remotely resembles the paint chip.

The first time this happened was when I decided I wanted our living room and dining room walls painted the cool celery green I remembered as a child in my great-grandma Jensen's house. Every time we visited her elegant home—so unlike the succession of inexpensive rentals we lived in growing up—I was struck by the beauty of the pale celery green walls and crisp white crown molding.

Nearly forty years later, I wanted to recapture that fresh, cool elegance in my own home. Unfortunately, when I dipped my paint brush into the first can of paint, instead of the light celery green I yearned for, what wound up on the walls was more of an ocean blue.

A cold Atlantic ocean. There was no warmth to the blue at all.

But since I, like my pal Jan, have an impatient nature and just want to get the project done rather than spending many more hours and days trying to recapture the exact shade of green from my memory, I decided instead to go to plan B: soft butter yellow.

So Michael trotted off to the hardware store and came back with yellow paint instead. And now everyone who comes over and sees the pale yellow against the marshmallow-white crown molding loves it and asks, "What's your paint color?"

When Michael and I, along with our friend Karen, went over one weeknight to our friend Shane's house to help him paint his living room and study, it was with the best of intentions.

Over the past few months, Shane had run into countless problems with shoddy workers and subcontractors who never showed up when they said they would, so his house, which he was in the midst of having remodeled, was, to put it bluntly, a mess with torn-up rooms and half-finished jobs left and right.

Not to mention a severely stressed-out friend who'd reached the end of his remodeling rope.

So we three pitched in. Michael headed for the study to painstakingly paint the built-in floor-to-ceiling bookcase, while Karen and I decided to make quick work of the living room.

Unlike many of my girlfriends, I really enjoy painting. There's nothing quite like the feeling I get when slapping fresh paint on a huge expanse of white wall and then rolling it in all directions. I think it unleashes my frustrated Rembrandt tendencies.

> There's nothing quite like the feeling I get when slapping fresh paint on a huge expanse of white wall and then rolling it in all directions. I think it unleashes my frustrated Rembrandt tendencies.

Or at least Jackson Pollock.

Eagerly I picked up a roller, dipped it in the paint, and was ready to go.

Or so I thought.

Shane stopped me and directed my attention to this strange-looking plastic thingy with dozens of little holes standing in the oversized paint drum. It resembled nothing so much as a giant cheese grater. I'd never before seen such an exotic paint accessory.

"What you want to do is rub the roller up and down on this several times to get the excess paint off so it won't drip." Shane demonstrated.

So much for my quick painting fix to help out my pal. Can you say time consuming? And tiring?

Naively I'd imagined it would be a paint-by-numbers piece of cake. It's not like it's brain surgery or anything, and Karen and I had both painted dozens, if not hundreds, of times before.

Just never for our perfectionist friend.

We teased Shane about his scrupulous and oh-so-precise attention to every aspect of the painting process, but he said, "Well, this is my home, a representation of who I am. I know you'd want the same thing in your house, wouldn't you?"

"Nope," I said. "I'd just want it done so I could relax with a good book. Besides, that's what furniture and pictures are for—to cover up the mistakes."

Although Shane was quite touched by our gesture and grateful for the help, I also have the sneaking suspicion that after we left that night he came around behind us and did a lot of touch-up. (Except where Michael painted, since he and Shane are of the same meticulous mettle.)

Then there's my uncle Jimmy.

When he retired, he decided he'd paint all the bedrooms in his and Aunt Sharon's house. But he got sidetracked by other things—golf, morning coffee with his brothers, and televised sports—so he didn't get it done right away.

Then my grandpa, Aunt Sharon's dad, got sick and was taken to the hospital, so Sharon spent all her free time visiting Grandpa at the hospital and making sure he had everything he needed. One day during one of her visits, Jimmy decided to surprise his wife and finally paint the bedrooms as a treat for her.

When Sharon got home and walked into their bedroom, she couldn't believe her eyes. The walls were bright sky blue. Not a soft, robin's egg blue but a vivid, overwhelming, in-your-face bluebird blue.

She'd had in mind more of a subtle beige.

"At first I didn't want to say too much about it," Sharon said, "but it's still that color today. Jimmy said he brought a color chart home, but I don't remember ever seeing it."

Another time Jimmy painted an inside door. "He decided not to put the top back on the paint can in the hallway, so the door swung and hit him, and paint fell all over," Aunt Sharon recalled. "He was in paint from here to New York."

Early in their marriage they had a cute bright red table that fit perfectly in the kitchen in their first apartment—if Sharon took the leaf out. She'd recently given birth to her first child, my cousin Scott, and told Uncle Jimmy she really needed a shelf in the pantry, just big enough to put all the baby food on so it didn't keep getting lost with the canned soup and vegetables.

"I came home and a shelf was up, and I was so happy and thrilled," Sharon recalled. About a month later they decided to have her mom and dad over for supper one night, and she asked Jimmy, "Where's the leaf to the table?"

"He pointed to the pantry and said, 'That's your new shelf.' He'd painted it!" Sharon said. "He's not too handy, so we usually hire things out."

My girlfriend Laurie said that after she married Tom and moved into his house, they definitely needed to paint it, but she also had an ulterior motive: "to get rid of all the awful artwork he had collected over the years—before we met—at various art and wine festivals. There were photos in baby-blue mats and '70s frames, an African batik-type print in a leopard frame, and tiny engravings from Europe from when he went there with his ex-wife years ago. One of my more 'sleuthy' neighbors gave me the idea. 'Just take all the paintings down and paint. Then hide those pictures and talk vaguely about redecorating or rearranging the pictures. If he still doesn't notice after three months, throw them in the trash or store them out of sight in the attic.'

"And that's what I did," Laurie said. "Worked like a charm."

She said the first room they attacked was an eye-opener. "The dining room had this grass-like wallpaper on the walls, but it had been painted over with beige semigloss paint. The result was that it looked like the walls were moldy with dark bits of fuzz showing through. I estimated that it wouldn't take but an evening to get the wallpaper off," Laurie recalled. "I said this on Friday evening, and Tom warned me that he had done this sort of project before and it would probably take a bit longer. I told him he didn't know what he was talking about. Days later we discovered yet a *third* layer of wallpaper underneath that we were trying to chip off the walls.

"We hired someone to finish it, and I learned to not blow off my husband's opinion even though he doesn't know his way around a hammer," Laurie said with a fond smile.

For their bedroom, my friend had the "misguided idea" to paint the walls a rosy, warm coral color. Laurie bought all new furniture in a cream color to offset her idea and hired a painter to create a faux finish. "It ended up looking like someone threw up Pepto-Bismol all over the walls and then rolled in it," she recalled. "It was like being on one of those medical shows where they put a camera inside a person's body and show you what's going on deep inside where you shouldn't be looking. Tom walked in the front door that night and said, 'How's the room?'"

As Laurie ushered her husband into the bedroom, he said, "Or should I say *womb*?"

Deborah, my former co-worker who moved to Florida, said her husband, Gene, told her he'd be glad to paint the bathroom for her. After all, he loves to paint.

And so he began.

"Honey, would you please get me a drop cloth?"

"Hey, babe, this would go much faster if you could mask the trim off for me. Won't take you ten minutes."

"Oh, I've got all the trim cut in. Could you just wash this brush out for me?"

"I'm finished. How does it look? I need to put this ladder away—how about rinsing the roller out?"

"When friends come over," Deborah said, "he's right there with, 'How do you like the bathroom? I painted it myself!'"

Maria, who moved from Sacramento to South Dakota, said she tried her husband's patience with paint.

Living out in the middle of the South Dakota countryside, the nearest place to buy paint where you could "color match" with fabric, dishes, etc., was sixty-five miles away. "I'm not that good of a visualizer when it comes to those small patches," Maria said, "so I needed to buy a few (hundred) small cans of paint in the color type I thought I might like. Okay, it wasn't

51

a hundred; it was more like ten. But Ralph always wondered exactly how many shades of 'cherry mocha' I was going to try. He thought 'the first one' was always okay.

"Although he did say my final set of colors were 'brilliant,' and they were."

When our friends Bill and Andrea moved into their charming, older home in an established, well-to-do area of the community, painting was one of the first things they did.

Initially, Andrea decided that she wanted to go with a soft green palette, so she bought varying shades in quart cans and painted sections of the wall to decide which green she liked the best. Then came the day she visited a friend's house and saw the elegant taupe color she'd painted her walls. On her way home, Andrea made a quick detour to the paint store for a couple more quarts to dab on different shades of taupe next to the green.

When Bill got home that night, he took one look, yelled for Andrea to "Get down!", pointed both his hands, and made the rat-a-tat sound of a machine gun at the camouflage wall.

It did the trick. Andrea finally settled on a mustardy yellow, which they just finished painting in the living room before the holidays, but they didn't have time to put up the white crown molding or baseboard before Christmas.

Bill's mother came to visit for the holidays and said, "Oh, I remember these horrendous colors from the seventies, this baby-poop yellow—won't you be happy to change it and make it white?"

Andrea smiled sweetly at her mother-in-law and said, "That *is* the right color."

But my friend had just begun to paint.

The couple wound up painting their kitchen three times. "I had the blues computer generated," Andrea recalled, "a blue in a teacup I liked, a blue in the ginger jar I liked, and then I tried to match a blue scarf, but none of them was exactly right."

Finally, in frustration, Bill gave up and mixed the three blues together. The couple now has a striking cobalt blue kitchen with white bead-board cabinets, flecked granite countertops, and a slate floor that has been featured in the Interiors section of their local newspaper a couple times.

Lonnie and her husband, Joe, have never painted a room in their lives.

"We still haven't," Lonnie said. "When we moved into this big, old farmhouse, David, one of our really handy friends, looked everything over, then said, 'So what color are you going to paint the living room?'"

"David, the living room *is* painted."

It hadn't occurred to Lonnie to put her own paint on the walls, and it wouldn't have occurred to David that one could actually live with the previous owner's paint job.

"Joe and I decided that twenty years of renting must have affected us deeply," Lonnie said. "We had low homeowner's self-esteem."

Not to worry, Lonnie. Next time I come to visit, I'll be glad to help you paint. Just as long as you don't look too closely at the edges.

---

*By wisdom a house is built, and through understanding it is established.*

—PROVERBS 24:3

# 4

# waging a wallpaper war

...

*We'd been told that the couple that spack-
les together cackles together. They lied. In
our house, hanging wallpaper was no
laughing matter.*

Michael and I have only wallpapered together once.
That's all it took.

And it wasn't even an entire room, just one wall
in the kitchen. But we were ready to tear each other limb
from limb by the time we'd finished, or at the very least
shred the infamous wallpaper into a thousand tiny pieces.

I think it has something to do with our differing personality types.

Much has been written by those far more expert than
me on the subject of personality types—sanguine, melan-

cholic, phlegmatic, choleric; otter, lion, golden retriever, yadda yadda yadda—which I won't repeat here. You've read the books, and if you haven't, you probably need to, even if it's just a quick skim.

But what *I'm* talking about are the different home-improvement project personality types.

Michael falls under the methodical, think-it-through, precise, slow, tape-measuring type, while I land squarely atop the hurry-up-and-get-it-done, as-long-as-it-looks-pretty, impatient type list.

Not a very good working combination. And certainly not conducive to candlelight and sweet pillow talk later. Which is why the next time a room in our house needed to be wallpapered, I called up my best friend Lana, and together we decided to surprise Michael.

My husband was definitely surprised and pleased when he came home that night and saw the delicate pink-and-green rosebud pattern on a creamy background with its complementary border on the wall behind our bed.

But a year later when we had to move the bed to the opposite wall to install two new wall-mounted reading lights, he was a little less pleased.

"What happened there?" he said, pointing to a fifteen-inch section of blank wall above the baseboard.

"Oh, that. I'd forgotten all about that," I said. "When Lana and I were wallpapering last year, we mismeasured on that one strip, and it looked like we were going to run out of wallpaper, so we left that spot bare and agreed to come back and fix it once we finished the wall—if there was any paper left," I explained.

"Well, was there any paper left?"

"Yep, but by the time we finished, we were both so hot and tired from all the work we'd done, and Lana had to get home, so I decided I'd fix it later. But then I forgot all about it since the bed covered it up."

My husband shook his head in amused disbelief as we finished moving the bed. Then we had to rearrange the dressers, and his amusement turned to incredulity.

"What's that?" he said, pointing to a smaller four-inch section of blank wall at the bottom of the last wallpaper panel.

"Oh, that's another place where we were a little off on our measuring and ran short again. But, honey, it doesn't matter; it's going to be covered up by the coat rack. No one will ever see it."

He raised his eyebrows at me. "Where's the rest of the wallpaper?"

"In the garage, I think."

A couple minutes later, Michael had covered over the blank spots. But he didn't even bother to measure, just took out the scissors and cut freehand!

I was shocked.

He smiled. "This from the woman who left blank spots on the wall in two places for more than a year?"

**My pal Jan considers herself the wallpaper queen.**

My pal Jan considers herself the wallpaper queen.

"Only trouble is, I don't do math, so I can never figure out how much to buy," she admitted.

She knows you can get the experts to figure it out for you, but for that, you have to have the proper wall dimensions. Jan says she bought borders for their bedroom, and they didn't get around to putting them up for three years. "Finally, we tackled the project. Fortunately, I had stashed the borders in a place where I could remember," Jan said. "We got nearly done and ran out of paper." Luckily, they shop at a local paint store that keeps records of their purchases. The salesclerk at the store found the name of the border and discovered it was still in stock, so they were able to order more.

These days, however, Jan has a bad neck and can't slap the paper on the walls like the pro she used to be. She can't poise her neck in the up position for too long. But she loves the ambience of a wallpapered room. "So Carl does it, and I just order him around," Jan said. "'Honey, there's too much glue on that one. Hurry up, it's drying too fast,' I'll say. Then he reminds me of the Victorian again. 'Every room was wallpapered, you know.' Translation: 'I know what I'm doing, so keep quiet.'"

But Jan can't stand to just observe when it comes to this creative endeavor, so she sneaks up on the ladder to rub out the bubbles and reposition the paper just right while he's in the kitchen wetting down the next roll.

Carl returns and gives her an admonishing look. "Jan, you're going to wake up with a neck ache tomorrow. Is it worth it?"

And Jan's plaintive reply?

"But Carl, I need *something* to do. I'll just pop some more aspirin and pray."

She's hopeless, but the house is quite cute.

Katie, my now-country girlfriend, admits that she used to complain and wonder why the previous homeowners did halfhearted jobs around the house, but she quickly changed her attitude. "When we started putting new windows and wall coverings in, I realized, *We're desperate. Just do anything to finish the project!*" Katie said. "We always think the others before us just messed up and didn't know what they were doing. Like when we took all the wallpaper down and discovered paneling beneath it: 'What were they thinking?' As you get a little bit educated, you start being less judgmental," she confessed. "They were thinking they wanted to actually be able to pay the mortgage, so they stopped repairing."

Which is the same reason Mark and Katie wound up painting over that same paneling.

Andrea, my trendy, upscale girlfriend, had the bathroom of my dreams. Years ago, when she and Bill first moved into their charming cottage fixer-upper, she had the hall bathroom professionally wallpapered in an exquisite blue-and-white toile—long before toile became so popular.

It was one of the most gorgeous bathrooms I'd ever seen, and I loved spending time in there admiring the pretty pattern of blue birds and flowers above the gleaming white bead board.

But recently my friend decided she was burnt out on toile and it was time to make a change. Andrea had some other wallpaper she'd purchased a while before and decided to once again hire the job out. Unfortunately, she'd miscalculated, and the professional wallpaperer informed her she didn't have enough rolls to redo the bathroom. Since she'd bought the paper five years before, it was now out of stock, and they couldn't find any more.

So Bill and Andrea started schlepping all over town to different wallpaper stores to search for something new—with Andrea hunting and Bill mostly sleeping. Finally she gave up. She couldn't find any wallpaper she wanted, so she decided to go with paint instead.

Initially, the couple had painted over the existing wallpaper to prime it for the new, but now, since they were painting instead, they had to strip off all the old wallpaper. "We spent ten hours together stripping the wallpaper," Andrea recalled, "and wound up pulling parts of the wall out. It was a real test of our marriage."

Afterward, Bill had to replaster the entire bathroom and then paint it. "It's now a lovely restoration green and white," Andrea told me.

I'm sure it is. But I have yet to see it, because I'm still in mourning for the blue-and-white toile.

My friend Peggy has the wallpapering-with-your-husband story to end all wallpapering stories.

"You know how it is when you have it on the calendar to tackle a project on a particular weekend, and no matter what, you're going to get it done?" she asked me.

Of course. What woman doesn't?

Well, several years ago, Peggy had saved Memorial Day weekend (three whole days!) to wallpaper and paint their master bedroom. "I was determined it would be done that weekend," she recalled. "Did it really matter that Curt had to have knee surgery the week prior to that and had his leg in an immobilizer? As long as he could climb a stepladder with one good leg while the other one stuck out at a forty-five-degree angle, we would get the project done."

Her still-recuperating husband had to hop up and down the ladder with his one good leg to hold the wallpaper strip from the top while Peggy straightened it from the bottom—all the way around the room.

"Poor Curt," his wife said. "I feel more than a little sheepish now about how my obsession to get the job done on that particular weekend probably caused my sweet husband lots of discomfort. But he never complained.

"And we got it done—and it looked really nice too."

*She watches over the affairs of her household*
*and does not eat the bread of idleness.*

—PROVERBS 31:27

# 5

# puttin' out the drips

...

*When it rains, it pours.*
*Stories of leaky situations.*

As you know, my friends Jan and Carl are the proud owners of a little cabin-in-the-woods getaway. Every winter the pipes under the cabin would break. They'd discover it in late spring when they opened up the cabin for the summer season and had no water.

"Where was help when I needed it?" Jan asked, chuckling. "It was a two-man job to repair broken pipes. I had to crawl under the cabin and hold the blow torch for half an hour while Carl attempted repairs on new copper fittings he was sure would solve the problem," my friend recalled. "For four years we repeated this scenario. Carl ignored my whining about hiring an expert. After all, he'd repaired all the pipes in the Victorian. He knows about pipes. In such close quarters, I didn't remind him that those pipes did not live in harsh winter conditions. I kept quiet and readjusted my body a bit, only to roll over on a limp, warm piece of fur—a very recent victim of one of the multiple boxes of D-Con mouse bait strategically placed in the cabin.

"That was it," Jan said. "I called a plumber that afternoon. He explained that the pipes would never drain properly because they were old and saggy; water would always get trapped, freeze, and burst the pipes. Every year."

So Jan said those two magic words that roll off every homeowner's tongue when all else fails: "Fix it." And he did. They now have new copper pipes under the cabin, constantly warmed by electricity so they will never freeze, and nice shut-off valves inside the cabin so nobody has to dig in the snow to find them anymore.

But for some reason, Jan can't get any takers on a tour of the heated pipes. Even if they did cost more than those new doors. Sorry.

Jan, let me stop right here and say that you're a far better woman than me. I wouldn't/couldn't have gone under the cabin in the first place, and had I somehow been able to work up the courage to quell my claustrophobia, Mr. Mouse would have sent me running right to a motel.

Aside from the under-the-cabin problem, Jan said that the inside pipes would often burst because their guests would forget to put antifreeze in the toilet. "So every year without fail, in early spring we'd come up to the cabin to a broken john," she said. "Trouble is, the closest place to get a new one is forty-five minutes away."

One spring, however, rather than Jan and Carl taking their usual getaway, Jan decided to have some girl time with her best friend Jeanne instead, and when they arrived at the cabin, once again the commode was broken. Although Jan is quite the wonder-woman handygirl, even she didn't know how to replace an entire toilet yet—although she'd helped Carl properly "seat" the toilet ring many times. This time she knew it would be fruitless to make the forty-five-minute drive to buy a new toilet that she wouldn't be able to install.

If it were city-girl wuss me, I probably would have given up at that point and headed for the nearest motel. But not the intrepid country girls Jan and Jeanne. Instead, they used a chamber pot for four days and pretended they were Laura and Mary Ingalls at their little house on the prairie.

When my Ohio friend Joyce and her husband, Dan, moved into their "new" house, they discovered the former owners had been smokers. "When we viewed the house, the windows were open and it didn't smell," Joyce recalled. But the first time she closed the bathroom door and climbed in the tub for a nice, relaxing bath, she nearly gagged from the smell emanating from the white paneling on the wall.

So while her husband was at work, she pulled all the paneling down. "Great idea, except that beneath the paneling was yellow paint and psychedelic wallpaper," she said. "The former owners had glued the paneling, and removing the paneling removed chunks of the wall. At this point we decided that while we were at it, we might as well add a shower, since the bath only had a tub.

"Then we decided we might as well replace the fixtures too. And the flooring."

Fast forward: The sink and toilet were out, and Dan wanted to remove the tub, but they thought it was cast iron. "I asked him to please call his dad to come and help, because

I didn't want him to hurt himself," Joyce said. Dan called his dad but then discovered that the tub wasn't cast iron, just enameled steel. "I can do this by myself!" he shouted as he gave the tub a pull. As he pulled, he sheared off the water supply for the toilet. Suddenly, water was shooting up five feet into the air. "Since we had concrete slab floors, the water was fast approaching the carpeting in the hallway," Joyce recalled.

> **Suddenly, water was shooting up five feet into the air.**

They put a barricade of towels and clothes at the bathroom doorway to try to keep the water from encroaching on the hallway carpet. But the water went *under* the wall into the kitchen. "I went running outside to the shutoff valve, but when I got there I discovered that not only did the shutoff have no handle but the stub was stripped because people had used pliers on it so many times. Dan was inside trying to do what he could, I called the city water department, and then he finally remembered the main shutoff at the street. He was just turning it off when the city water truck arrived."

The completed bathroom had a new tub, vanity, and toilet, plus a ceramic tile floor and walls tiled five feet tall around the entire bath. Joyce told me, "After I was done with the tile job, Dan vaguely said, 'I don't think I tested the new water line behind the wall . . .'"

Lonnie and Joe live in a house that is high and dry and sits on a knoll with no swamp nearby. "Never ever did the basement leak," Lonnie said, "and my husband was telling the appraiser that very thing as they walked down the basement stairs and into the . . . water."

Turns out that earlier in the day, the gutter guy had used an outdoor water spout to hose out the gutters, and for some reason, the water from that spout backed into the basement and just kept going and going and going. "None of us realized it," Lonnie said. "The gutter guy went home, the appraiser man arrived, the husband gave him the tour, and voilà, the first and only time we had a flood."

In the process of adding an addition to their old farmhouse, my cousins Barb and Frank had to have the basement redone as well. Finally the basement was finished, painted, and ready to go, complete with brand-new shelving that had just been installed. "Frank went down early one morning to check on the basement, since it had rained the night before," Barb recalled. "I heard a lot of expletives coming up from the basement stairwell. The room had six inches of mucky water in it. Turns out the sump pump wasn't working. There went more money. Additionally, the varnish on the bottom shelves had to be completely redone. More bucks."

Johnny and Jeannie have also had some interesting plumbing challenges in their gorgeous three-story Victorian home.

Early on they had to remove a four-hundred-pound claw-foot tub from the main bathroom because his mother had difficulty getting in and out of it and they wanted to replace it with a shower. "It almost killed me, sliding down the back steps," Johnny recalled.

Additionally, one day in their multi-year remodel of the old house, Johnny was finishing removing a washer and dryer from the former back porch to make room for a round staircase that would connect the basement with the middle floor. In the process, he noticed a crawl space opening with a door up near the ceiling. Johnny had noticed it before, but hadn't been able to get to it with the appliances in the way. With the washer and dryer now gone, he climbed up on a ladder and opened the door that showed some of a remodel done in 1920 to change the configuration of the house.

Much to Johnny's shock and dismay, however, when he looked to the side where the plumbing ran down from the top floor bathroom, he saw that only the bottom half of the pipes remained! The top part of all the pipes had completely corroded away, leaving open pipes that resembled troughs. This meant that the sewage and water from the sink, bath, and toilet was flowing through half-corroded-away pipes. "We'd lived in the house for nearly a year and never knew this," Jeannie said. "Needless to say, our plumber had a huge job replacing all the plumbing from the top story—he had to work in a very small crawl space. He wasn't happy, but we were thankful that Johnny looked into the opening before a major disaster occurred!"

Johnny also made an interesting discovery when he was remodeling the upstairs bath (formerly the kitchen). He had to take up the floor to run new plumbing, and in the floor—which was also the second floor ceiling—he found an ancient, but completely intact, bottle of whiskey brewed in Sacramento.

Pastor Johnny didn't imbibe, however, even though the whiskey was finely aged.

---

*Man proposes, but God disposes.*

---

—*Thomas à Kempis*

# 6

# time to buy stock in home depot

• • •

*It was just a quick trip to the do-it-yourself
store for a box of nails. One hour and more
than two hundred dollars later, we finally
escaped. We couldn't even drive past
the hardware store without paying
a triple-digit toll.*

Barb said she and her husband, Frank, felt they had a
room of their own at Home Depot, they went there
so often. "Our car went on autopilot every time we
left the house," she said.

I hear that.

The first year we lived in our house, it seemed we spent
every weekend and every last dollar at Home Depot.

We'd go in for a $1.47 box of nails and leave an hour
later with tools I didn't know we needed, screws, plants,

and a plethora of other home-improvement must-haves that always wound up in the triple digits.

We've decided they must have some special code hooked up to the cash registers that scans when a first-time home-owner comes in so that it knows to never register in the double digits but rather a minimum of a hundred dollars each time. (Although we've since learned from talking to other friends that it's not just new homeowners who run the Home Depot triple-digit marathon.)

My friend Jill, whom I first met when she was my sixth-grade teacher in Racine, Wisconsin, decades ago, knew for the past few years that she needed new carpeting in the house she'd been living in for more than thirty years. However, her elderly mother, whom she lived with, had to use a walker to get around, and the disruption of tearing out the old, worn-out carpeting and replacing it with new would have been too hard on her. So Jill put the project on hold.

One night as Jill was watching TV a few months after her mother had passed away, she couldn't stand it anymore and decided the time had come to replace the carpet.

Immediately.

But she dreaded the thought of going out to several stores to find what she wanted, so she chose a small family-owned carpet store instead—the same store that had put the present carpet in some thirty-six years ago. With the assistance of a friend and the store owner's wife, Jill made several trips to and from the carpet store with samples of various shades of beige and caramel brown—checking all the samples under various light conditions and trying to match her furniture and paint hues.

Finally she settled on a light caramel brown to carpet the living room, dining room, hallway, and three bedrooms.

However, the more Jill looked at the sample, the more she realized that painting would be necessary to pull it all together. The living room would be fine; it just needed some cleaning and touch-up. "I'd always gotten Sears paint," Jill recalled, "but when I got there, I found out our Sears store hasn't carried paint for two years."

Instead, she headed to Home Depot—just the first of many trips.

First, Jill painted the three bedrooms, which made them look fresh and clean. But then the hall looked a bit dingy and needed some lightening up. To paint the hall, she had to paint the kitchen as well, because they share a common wall.

Back to Home Depot again for more paint.

Now the hall bathroom looked really dated.

Back to Home Depot again with the well-used credit card.

Then the old metal and plastic shower door looked tacky, so off to the department store.

"After giving the credit card a really good workout there—shower curtain, liner, rod, hangers, new sets of towels, soaps, and tissue box—I knew the bathroom now wouldn't detract from the rest of the redo," Jill said.

> **Back to Home Depot again with the well-used credit card.**

Yet the more she looked at the nice rug sample and new paint, Jill's furniture started to look a bit worn and in need of an upgrade. So off to a specialty Amish furniture store in Milwaukee. "It was a rainy Saturday morning—what else did I have to do?" she said.

Within two hours, which Jill says was a record for her because she's not usually so impulsive, she found a new sofa and ordered chairs in contrasting colors to go with it. She also found two new bedroom sets with headboards, dressers, and nightstands. Her credit card got another good workout.

But when she got home, her old end tables looked outdated to her. "I had painstakingly retouched them with these wonderful furniture markers so they weren't really bad—just outdated in relation to all my brand new furniture."

Back to the Amish store, where she got five new tables that, thankfully, had been marked down.

Only now the kitchen table set looked really shabby. Off to a huge furniture store in Milwaukee the next rainy Saturday for a new table and chairs.

Jill couldn't wait for her new carpet to be laid.

Except that no one had mentioned that when you get new carpeting, all the room and closet doors may need some adjusting for height. "Not one door would go back on," Jill recalled. "It seems my old, worn carpeting was lower than my new padding alone. So there I was with wonderful new plush carpeting and no doors on the rooms or closets. They were all standing out in my garage." Not being a carpenter, she thought, *What now?*

Jill happened to see her neighbor across the street and asked his advice. Turns out his nephew was a "husband for hire" who did odd handyman jobs. However, after talking to him, Jill learned that he was unable to help her fix the doors for another two months or so.

Instead, she headed back to her home away from home, Home Depot, to price new doors, thinking that it might be a good idea to just replace them as well. But the new doors were longer than the ones she already had and still needed to be cut down and rehung.

"I mentioned my dilemma to my dear younger brother, and I must have sounded desperate enough, for he promised to tackle the job," Jill recalled.

Back to Home Depot to get a saw blade for cutting interior veneer doors. "The guy guaranteed us that the one he recommended would do the job neatly," she said. "But the blade we tried really splintered the first door, which still looks pretty rough at the moment."

Once they got the hang of it and accidentally turned the door to the back side up and cut, things got better, Jill said. Not perfect, but better. Although she still has to find a way to cosmetically treat the doors—she's still working on that.

After all these home-improvement projects were completed, it dawned on Jill that with her new bed arriving the next day, it would really be nice to have some bedding to put on it.

Off to Sears for a new comforter, dust ruffle, sheets, and pillow cases.

"What started out as a need for new carpeting has become an adventure in itself," Jill said, laughing.

And the adventure still continues. After Jill got all her new furniture, she couldn't believe it was the same house she'd lived in for the past four decades. Only now she's decided that the computer room looks really cluttered, so she's off to find a nice wood cabinet and do a little more rearranging, which she realizes will require another trip to the Amish store to get a small TV table for her bedroom.

"Thank heaven school is starting," Jill said. "It will keep me out of furniture and home-improvement stores."

When Jan and Carl were first married, their romantic date nights always took place at Home Depot. "We did buy stock, by the way, so it softens the shock of the cash register receipt," Jan said.

> **When Jan and Carl were first married, their romantic date nights always took place at Home Depot.**

"Each date was at least two hours long, because Mr. Meticulous has to comb every aisle to complete his list of every screw, bolt, nut, and light switch we need," she recalled. "I usually go search through wallpaper books for ideas and can never find him when I'm done. One time after hiking three miles up and down the aisles, I went home grumbling about how we lose each other in that monstrous store, so we bought walkie-talkies. Most people use them at fairs and events; we use them to find each other at Home Depot. It's great!"

Jan pushes her talk switch when it comes time to search for Carl: "Where *are* you?"

"I'm in plumbing supplies, right next to the p-traps."

Hmm, maybe Michael and I should consider investing in walkie-talkies. Except he always knows just where to find me: in the kitchen area, drooling over cupboards and countertops and turning green with kitchen envy.

---

*The fellow that owns his own home is always just coming out of a hardware store.*

—Frank McKinney Hubbard

# 7

# the worker waltz (aka the subcontractor slow dance)

• • •

*Welcome to the Renovation Twilight Zone,*
*where workers live in a parallel universe*
*and time as you know it will never be*
*the same again.*

New homeowners are babes in the renovating woods when it comes to the world of contractors and home-improvement workers.

I naively assumed it was just like any other work environment—someone is hired to do a job, he comes out and does good work in a timely fashion, you pay him, and everyone's happy. But what I and many of my novice homeowner friends didn't realize is that the world of contractors and subcontractors is a different universe all its own—with its own peculiar timetable.

Which I quickly learned the first time we had to call an electrician to come out and do some wiring for us.

> But what I and many of my novice homeowner friends didn't realize is that the world of contractors and subcontractors is a different universe all its own—with its own peculiar timetable.

We found a guy—a one-man operation—who was recommended by a friend for his reasonable rates. However, the friend also cautioned us that although the electrician was good, he was also sometimes difficult to reach.

I'll say.

It took three or four calls left on Mr. Electrician's answering machine over about a month-long period before we ever heard back from him.

When we finally did, he agreed to come out and give us an estimate in a couple days.

Which he did. And it was reasonable. Great. Then he started to leave.

"Aren't you going to start the wiring now?" I asked cluelessly.

"Oh no, not today. I've got a couple other jobs I'm doing; I just came out to bid this one."

Three weeks later, Electrical Man finally managed to fit us in and come out to do the work. Correction. To start the job.

He ran into some unexpected problems that required a trip to the nearby hardware store and took longer than he thought. Consequently, about halfway through the job, he had to leave because he had another appointment on the other side of town.

And the earliest he'd be able to return was four days later. Meanwhile, there was a hole in the ceiling of my office where our new ceiling fan would go. Oh, and by the way, when he was up in the attic running the wire from the electrical conduit thingamajig, he informed me that he found evidence that some mice had been making their home up there.

*Mice.* As in scurrying furry creatures with long tails. As in *not* the word you want to say to me. I know some people think that these little animals are cute and adorable, but not me. They're still a member of the rodent family—as in big, creepy rats and disease. Ugh. With visions of mice dropping onto my head while I worked, I made the electrician stuff a rag in the hole until his return.

And when Michael got home that night, he set some traps for his mice-scared wife.

Finally Mr. Electrical returned and finished the job. All told, it took nearly three months from when we first made the call to install two ceiling fans and a new light switch and to hook up another small switch in the garage to control the front yard sprinkler system.

We should have seen the writing on the contracting wall . . .

In addition to our ugly kitchen, I'd always hated our hideous hall bath with the avocado-pistachio wall tile; tan tub, toilet, and sink; and gray tile floor. We lived with the competing colors for a year or so until the toilet broke, at which time we replaced it with a brand-new gleaming white one. While we were at it, we figured we might as well replace the old wall-mounted beige sink with a white

75

vanity and attached cabinet, which would finally give us a place to store cleaning supplies and toiletries.

When I say "we," what I really mean is that we bought the new sink and toilet, but our wonderful plumber friend Michael Yarbrough (married to my best friend Lana) kindly came and installed them for us.

Michael is definitely a prince among plumbers. He shows up when he says he will, always does an excellent job, and maintains his happy, cheerful attitude while he works. Unfortunately, he's spoiled us for other workers. We thought everyone would possess the same hard-work ethic and dependability as him.

Not exactly.

A couple years after replacing the bathroom vanity, we decided to have the tub and tile resurfaced—much easier, cheaper, and faster than removing and replacing the cast-iron tub, which would have meant also tearing out and replacing the old tile.

And the worker waltz began all over again.

This time was a little better though. This guy (another one-man operation) came out to do the work just a couple days after giving us his bid. He had to tape off the walls, sink, toilet, and other fixtures before spraying his amazing tile resurfacing stuff, so for a couple days it looked like that scene near the end of *E.T.* where Elliot's house is under quarantine in all that plastic. Our worker even wore a mask like the federal agent in *E.T.*

And just like E.T. came back to life, so did my bathroom.

Now it was drop-dead gorgeous in all its sparkling whiteness. No more avocado-pistachio walls, tan tub, or gray floor warring with each other. And the gleaming white made the tiny room look so much bigger too. I was in bathroom heaven and had no problem presenting this worker a check for his completed and *great* job.

I also immediately went out and bought new towels, rugs, and a white lace shower curtain for my pretty new bathroom. But when Michael came home that night, he noticed a few blemishes in the tub and on the floor that I hadn't seen.

No problem. Miracle-tile man had promised that we had thirty days to spot any flaws or problems, which he would then fix for free.

The problem came when I called his number and got an answering machine message that said he was in Thailand for the next month.

I left a message asking him to call as soon as he returned.

A month passed and no call.

Uh-oh. Had he skipped town or gone out of business?

I called back and left another message.

Three weeks passed and still no reply.

Great. Now we were going to have to live the rest of our lives with these ugly, glaring blemishes in my pretty little bathroom. Either that or pay someone else to come and fix them.

Finally, in the middle of the fourth week of the second month, he returned my call. "Hi, just got back from Thailand. Was having such a great time I decided to extend my vacation another few weeks." Fortunately for us, he also extended his thirty-day warranty and came out two days later to fix the flaws. So we had a happy ending to our bathroom remodel.

Unfortunately, our friend Shane wasn't so lucky.

Shane, who had little cash, decided to hire a guy to refinish the hardwood floors in his 1930s art deco home. A guy he knew nothing about, save for the fact that he worked cheap and had done a decent sand-and-stain job for an equally cash-strapped friend of his.

It started with a phone call to "Fred the floor guy" (not his real name). Instead of Fred, however, Shane reached an impatient woman who said, "He don't live here anymore." Shane finally got Fred's new number and contacted him, and he seemed excited to have the work. They set a price and a start date.

The night before the start of the job, Shane cleared virtually his entire house of all furnishings, stashed everything in his tiny kitchen and garage, and then went to sleep on his mattress, which he'd pulled into the living room.

At 7 a.m. he was awakened by a knock on the front door. It was Fred—two hours early. "Oh, I don't have a watch, and I drive in from Stockton [an hour south of Sacramento]," he explained. Shane managed to send Fred away to a nearby coffee shop for an hour while he showered and dressed. *No big deal,* my friend thought. *Anyone can make a mistake. Although it certainly isn't the kind of thing I would do my first day at a job . . .*

When Fred returned, he also brought along a helper who claimed to know plenty about electrical work, so thinking himself thrifty, Shane hired the guy to install a couple new electrical outlets. Later he discovered the electrical guy had a drug problem. "I wondered why he kept running his jigsaw over the same four-inch patch of floor for half an hour," Shane recalled. "He was flying the friendly skies—on methamphetamines."

A few days later, Shane dropped by the house on his lunch hour to be greeted by the sight of Fred pacing around the driveway and back patio, talking crazy conspiracy stories. He insisted his ex-wife had sent out a team of middle-aged folks in minivans and station wagons to follow him to Sacramento all the way from his home in Stockton. Twelve cars in all, Fred claimed. He saw them picking up cell phones and talking to each other. And some of the people in the cars were still waiting for him in the parking lot just behind Shane's house.

Later two of Shane's neighbors dropped by to complain that Fred had threatened them, insisting they were part of his ex-wife's surveillance team. My friend, worried that this loose nut might go ballistic on him, made a call to Fred's house, hoping to catch his girlfriend and make some sense of the matter. She insisted that Fred was a good, decent guy who was just prone to the occasional delusional fit when he skimped on his meds.

"I'll have a talk with him, and that'll settle him right down," the girlfriend promised.

It worked. In no time at all, Fred was back on his meds and could now begin staining the floor the ebony color Shane wanted. Their agreement was that Fred would sand the floors down, then apply the stain and finish it off with a sealant.

Fred stained the bedroom, the study, the hall, and a four-foot wide strip that ran the length of the living room before he ran out of stain. Unfortunately, the stain came out "patchy," with light and dark places—"like someone took that fake tanning stuff and applied it unevenly to their body," Shane recalled. "Fred kept saying it was the wood; it *couldn't* be the stain."

So my friend asked his floor guy to sand down the black areas and restain them. It still didn't help; the more he sanded the shadowy areas, the blacker they became. Finally Shane insisted that Fred call for some expert advice. "He did," Shane recalled, "and the word came back—dry rot." My homeowner friend then pulled up a few floorboards near a wall where the previous owners had installed a walled aquarium, and there was definite evidence of dry rot.

After arming himself with a flashlight and a few prayers, Shane crawled beneath the house and found significant evidence of dry rot beneath the laundry room where the aquarium had been mounted. Then he had to put in a call to the inspection company that should have discovered the problem during the presale inspection of the house.

The company said they'd fix it free of charge, although it wound up taking them two weeks and three tries to do so. At last the bad boards in the subfloor were repaired or replaced.

Shane still felt uneasy about Fred's dry rot theory as it applied to the rest of the mess, however. He found another floor company in the yellow pages that specialized in stains and got a more likely explanation: Apparently the special ebony stain he wanted was tricky to use—like a whitewash, it sits atop the floor's surface instead of sinking into the wood, and it requires a lot of care and TLC when it's applied. "You're the third guy this month who's called complaining about a botched ebony stain job," the specialist told Shane.

Now out came the specialists, who had to take razor blades to cut out the mistakes Fred had made in the wood.

Three months later—and three times the money my friend had initially planned to spend—the floors were finally finished. Shane joked, "It's ludicrous. For that kind of money I should have just installed heated marble floors."

And that's just the beginning of his house saga.

Blessed with ballooning equity, Shane decided to take out a home-improvement loan to remodel the bathroom and the rest of his house and also wipe out some hefty credit card debt he'd accrued from house-related things in his first year of ownership.

Like a pricey, twice-done hardwood floor job.

At his credit union, he met a nice gal who helped him secure his loan and who also told him that her husband was an experienced contractor with time on his hands who also happened to work inexpensively.

The two words every homeowner longs to hear: *experienced* and *inexpensive*.

> **The two words every homeowner longs to hear: *experienced* and *inexpensive*.**

Shane promptly phoned her husband and set up a start date for the bathroom remodel. The two men agreed on a price that seemed reasonable, and two weeks later, the work began. Still stinging from his hardwood floor debacle, however, Shane said from the get-go that he wanted a smooth transaction this time around.

The contractor (we'll call him Miguel) put my friend at ease by saying, "Let me put it this way: You don't pay me until the work is done. Then you pay me only if you like it."

Shane happily gave Miguel the green light.

In short order, the toilet, vanity, sink, and all the tile in the shower and around his tub were torn out. With a gutless bathroom now before him, talk turned to my friend's desire for a new kitchen. While Shane had initially planned to do much of the kitchen work with the help of an experienced contractor uncle, Miguel said he had a surplus of guys working for him and he'd love the chance to put them on task—for a reasonable price, of course.

They hammered out the numbers, and within days two scruffy guys were in Shane's utility room and kitchen, tearing out cabinets, hammering out plaster, peeling away chicken wire, and in general, making an extraordinary mess of his house.

Meanwhile, Miguel started asking for money.

Money for supplies, which seemed reasonable, and money to pay for half of the work, which didn't sit as well with Shane. Trusting soul that my friend is, however, he ponied up half the cash, but he also sat down with Miguel and told him he thought there ought to be some sort of contract—an itemized list of all the work that was being done and a dollar-by-dollar breakdown of what each task was costing him. "I just want to know I'm getting a fair value for what I'm paying," Shane told his contractor.

Miguel, who from the very beginning had made much ado about being a trustworthy guy, didn't like what he intuited as a lack of trust on my friend's part. His partner, however, saw the reasonableness of Shane's request and passed over some sketchy details about money matters he'd been writing down since the beginning of the project.

In short order, Shane's kitchen was stripped down to the studs so that he could look straight up into the rafters of the attic, and all the while, the bathroom remained without sink, shower, or toilet. Since it was the only bathroom in the house, my friend had to find new and creative ways to meet the call of Mother Nature.

At this point, Miguel's partner, the one writing things down, quit.

Two weeks later, after repeated requests from Shane, the bathroom floor tile was finally installed. Yet to bathe—or do just about anything requiring water, for that matter—Shane had to use a pair of needle-nose pliers to turn the two copper stems sticking out of the wall where his faucet would eventually go.

After this, things came to a slow halt.

Weeks passed and my friend's shiny new pedestal sink still sat in its box, his kitchen cabinets collected dust in their cartons, and each morning he fumbled with pliers—another set since the needle-nose pair disappeared with the tile guys—so he could have water for coffee and washing up.

By now, Shane had paid Miguel the balance on all of the work—even though several major tasks needed to be completed. And Miguel and company were all missing in action.

"Whole weeks would go by where Miguel wouldn't appear," Shane recalled.

Throughout these prolonged absences, my friend would call his contractor regularly, and on the occasions where he'd actually pick up the phone, Miguel would promise to show up. On a Saturday, he'd promise to be there Monday. By Monday evening, he'd say he'd be there by Tuesday. On Wednesday morning, he'd say he'd be there at noon. At two, he said he'd arrive by four. By nightfall, still no Miguel.

Again and again Miguel offered times and dates and the occasional "I'll be there for sure" yet bailed a good four out of five times.

After a while, not a single word was kept and Shane was beside himself with unfinished remodeling anxiety. "At one point I was so stressed out about the money being gone and the house not being finished that I pulled up in my driveway and had to remind myself what city and state I lived in," my friend confessed.

Finally, Shane gave Miguel a list of ten things to do to finish up the project and made him sign it and promise to complete it all within two weeks.

Guess what?

Miguel flaked yet again and finally confessed to Shane that he thought he was having a nervous breakdown. Shane, who's a sensitive, almost-too-tender-hearted guy, told Miguel, "God loves you," and prayed for him over the phone.

Miguel then agreed to pay Shane back the money he owed him for not doing the job.

And he did. Well, most of it, anyway.

"Miguel wasn't a liar or a cheat," said my friend, who wants to believe the best of everyone, "but he was a flake, which is almost as bad."

Since then, a helpful neighbor of Shane's has come in and done a great job with his plaster and electrical work, and Shane has hired a licensed contractor to finish up the rest of his remodel.

Our friend is planning to have a celebratory housewarming party soon so we can all see his beautifully renovated home.

We can't wait, Shane. We'll bring the cheese and crackers.

When Bill and Andrea first moved into their 1940s cottage fixer-upper, Andrea thought she'd help out by taking care of the administrative details—getting the bids from all the contractors and then hiring the best one.

She settled on someone who was referred to her by a co-worker. This "contractor" told her he could do all the work they needed on the entire house, top to bottom. In six months. For only ten thousand dollars.

Thrilled, Andrea gave him three thousand dollars the first day he showed up for work and never saw him again. Afterward, she realized that the supposed contractor's discourse on alien abductions and Area 51, coupled with some obscene alien tattoos on his legs, should have tipped her off.

Bill then stepped in and took over the worker-hiring duty. "We call it the '$3K remodel, gift with purchase' project, since this joker left behind a handheld sander valued at $29.95," Andrea said.

My cousin Debbie and her husband, Roy, did all the contractor work themselves when they built their dream house in the Texas countryside, but Roy hired subcontractors to do the brick work, electrical, etc., so Debbie's fully aware of the subcontractor slow dance.

"They'd show up and then disappear," she said wonderingly.

A homeowner friend of my cousin tried to warn her. "Debbie," she said, "contractors are like dogs. They come and they mark their territory, and then they're gone and nobody else will go near it. You can't get anyone else 'cause they know you've done a verbal handshake."

But Debbie thought, *Surely it can't be that hard.*

She quickly learned that it was after Roy had to fire a couple subcontractors for not showing up for weeks on end. "You have to be really careful and set deadlines, because most of them have ten or fifteen jobs going on at once,"

Debbie said. "Once they showed up, the work was great—it was just trying to get them back on the job site!"

When my Minnesota cousin Bettie and her husband, Stacy, were having their house remodeled, Bettie said the one thing that really got on her nerves was having workers in and out of her house practically all summer long. "I had to get up mighty early just to take a shower before everyone started to arrive," she recalled. "Forget watching the news, reading, or tuning in to an easy listening radio station. The crew brought their own entertainment—hard rock, at an ear piercing decibel, no exceptions."

She also learned an important lesson she wanted to pass on to other parents. "It's best to encourage your children to play far away from home unless you want them to catch an earful of the creative language that is spilled forth when things aren't working right or a problem arises," Bettie said. "And I thought army guys were bad . . ."

Yet I don't want to tar all contractors and subcontractors with the same brush. For every negative worker experience, there's an equal number of positive ones. Well, maybe the ratio isn't exactly the same, but remember, I'm bad with numbers. Close enough.

Take our carpenter friend Mike, for instance. My husband, Michael, and I knew him from our singles days at church but hadn't seen him in a few years. He'd married Rebecca, an old girlfriend of mine, and I'd heard through the grapevine that they'd had three or four kids. We'd also heard through the same grapevine that Mike was a whiz at installing crown molding.

Having just finished painting our living room and dining room a soft, pale butter color, we decided the walls needed bright white crown molding as an accent to make the rooms "pop." Only problem was, we didn't have a clue as to how to even *begin* installing our brand-new Home Depot crown molding.

Mike to the rescue.

Even though we hadn't seen each other in some time, when we called him, he immediately offered to come by the very next day and help us out.

The next afternoon Mike pulled up to our house with a very pregnant Rebecca in the front seat. "Great to see you!" I said, giving my old pal a hug as she clambered down from the truck. "So how many does this make now? Four? Or five?"

"Seven," she said, grinning.

"Wow. It *has* been a long time."

As Rebecca and I caught up, Mike and his teenage stepson Josh strapped on their tool belts, followed Michael inside, and went to work. And less than half an hour later, we had gorgeous crown molding rimming the perimeter of our living room and dining room! We couldn't believe it. Those guys sure knew how to use their nail guns.

Guess that's why they call them professionals.

Except Mike, the professional crown molding installer extraordinaire, refused to let us pay him for his help—even though he'd soon have a seventh mouth to feed. So to express our gratitude, we sent him and his family gift certificates to a favorite pizza parlor.

Then there was the time our friends Lana and Michael decided to have a pool installed in their backyard. They hired a subcontractor to pour the concrete, but first he had to install "coping"—a Styrofoam edge around the perimeter of the pool that the concrete would then be poured up against.

When Steve the subcontractor arrived to install the coping, it was late—nearly 8 p.m.—and he looked a bit the worse for wear, with dusty clothes and bloodshot eyes. So Lana didn't have the best first impression of him.

However, my friends soon learned he'd already worked twelve hours that day, hence the bloodshot eyes. The next morning, Steve arrived bright and early in his concrete truck—coincidentally at the same time another concrete truck pulled up to the next door neighbor's house—to pour Michael and Lana's cement. My best friend says he did a fabulous job, which immediately reversed her hasty first impression.

While he was waiting for my friends' concrete to set, Steve noticed that the neighbors—who'd chosen to go the do-it-yourself route and were pouring the cement on their own—were struggling with the difficult job, not sure exactly what they were doing. Good Samaritan Steve reached out and gave the neighbors the benefit of his professional expertise, not just telling them what to do but actually jumping right in and helping them do it correctly.

For free.

See. There are still good guys out there.

Michael, my best friend's plumber husband, is one of the best. He's one of the sweetest, most good-natured guys you'd ever meet—always ready and willing to help friends, family, co-workers, and his church whenever they're in plumbing need.

Michael refuses to take a dime for his efforts, although he's willing to trade labor. And those he helps out of sticky plumbing situations are only too happy to oblige.

More than a decade ago, our friends Pat and Ken needed the outside of their house painted. Not wanting to pick just anyone from the phone book at random, they asked the paint company for a list of professional painters, and Pat called and got several bids. A guy named Dave had the best bid and did "a fabulous job for a fair price," she recalled.

Some years passed and the couple needed some bits of painting done around the outside of the house—"the stuff that would make you crazy to do it all yourself," said Pat. Ken, the quintessential do-it-yourselfer, was getting a little older now—his upper fifties—and his body wasn't allowing him to do all the things he used to do easily ten or twenty years ago.

So remembering the good experience they'd had with Dave, Pat rummaged around, found his number again, and called to see if he was available.

By this point, Dave was in his midsixties and semiretired, since his wife was going through dialysis. But since it was just a three-day job and he wanted to help Pat and Ken out, Dave once again gave my friends a really good price and did an excellent job. "It's nice to know that there's still that quality of work around," Pat said.

Other friends swear by a local company that employs retired painters, electricians, carpenters, roofers, plumbers, glaziers, and all-around handymen. "They're great," our friends Jean and Jerry declared. "They come out promptly and give us an estimate, and if we accept it, they begin work right then and there—the very same day!"

Then there's my brother Dave, a gifted carpenter and skilled craftsman who helps build exclusive one-of-a-kind homes in northern California.

Once he and a crew of thirteen other workers were doing an extensive remodel of a house in an upscale neighborhood in Berkeley for a guy they'd worked for before and all liked and respected. The crew poured their hearts into the renovation and actually lived at the house for four months while they were remodeling. Every Thursday night, the homeowner's wife would cook a gourmet-style dinner for the hungry construction guys.

There was just one little problem.

Parking in the area was limited, and an elderly neighbor across the street would always yell at the workers for using *his* parking space. "That's *my* spot!" said the guy, who my brother said looked remarkably like Walter Matthau. "He was definitely a grumpy old man," Dave recalled. But the workers did their utmost to accommodate him, and my brother and his boss eventually won him over. "Within a month, his wife was making us pies and stuff," Dave said.

My girlfriend Annette's mom, Marolyn, did the same thing years ago when workers were building their dream home. "She wanted to keep the contractors happy, so she always baked them pies and cakes and brought homemade ice cream to the work site," Annette recalled. Not surprisingly, the construction workers did a wonderful job, and once the house was complete, Marolyn and her husband,

Louie, invited them all over for a celebratory barbecue to express their gratitude.

Then there's the flip side of the contractor coin.

My brother once helped remodel a home for a woman who had just retired from a top financial executive position, so she clearly had some bucks. "Her house was located on a gorgeous spot on five acres in the mountains," Dave recalled, "yet she had the contractor buy really cheap lumber for next to nothing. We wound up having to do a lot more milling on the wood just to get material that was usable."

After he and the other workers finally got the knotty pine conditioned to a point where they could use it, they began installing the wood around the windows, when the homeowner came by to inspect the progress.

Noticing a blue-gray streaky color in some of the wood—that occasionally appears, particularly in cheap lumber—the homeowner ordered that all the window trim that had just been put in be taken out and replaced. "No blue in the wood!" she insisted.

"Now we had even less material to work with," my brother recalled.

But the workers had the last say.

Using the rest of the inexpensive knotty pine for a breakfast nook with a bench seat, one of the carpenters snuck in a blue-gray board beneath the seat that the former high-powered executive would sit on but never ever see.

I think I'll remember to go the cake and pie route when we remodel our kitchen.

But my friend Lonnie's got the best contractor story of all. A romantic one, at that.

91

She and her new fiancé, Joe, announced their engagement one Christmas and planned a May wedding. Much happiness all around, until January. That's when they learned that Joe's mother was going to have her kitchen remodeled and the contractors had to start on February 1.

The date was not negotiable.

Lonnie says that Joe's mom is amazing when it comes to home improvements. "She drew up her own plans for dormer windows once, and when the contractor said there wasn't enough room because of the chimney, she said, 'Yes, there is. There will be a one-inch clearance.' And she was right. The contractor was stunned," Lonnie recalled. "She's impressively talented at this sort of thing, and she supervises workers well. I've always said that had she not had seven kids—and I'm sure glad she had Joe!—she would have been an engineer."

But when Lonnie found out that the contractors were starting February 1 and her soon-to-be mother-in-law couldn't leave in the middle of such a huge project to fly three time zones to their wedding, the bride-to-be gloomily predicted to her groom-in-waiting, "If our wedding plans are contingent on contractors' schedules, then we can't even *plan* a wedding until after the kitchen's done."

My friend knew whereof she spoke. She has vivid memories of her folks having their kitchen remodeled when she was a kid—the remodeling that was supposed to be done before the snow flew. "It wasn't," she said, "and the contractors worked all through the winter, during which we had to turn the heat off (think Michigan). We could never get warm during the day that year—not to mention having no kitchen all that time. And this predates microwave ovens!"

Her sweet husband-to-be came up with a great solution: "If the contractors are coming February 1, let's get married before they get there."

"That gave us three weeks to pull off a wedding, but we did it," Lonnie recalled. "We moved the date from sometime in May to January 30. It was a beautiful wedding, and we had a relaxed, all-day, family-only celebration, which set the tone for our combined family relationships from that day on. While it may have seemed like a bizarre reason to move a wedding day up by several months, today we're both glad it happened that way.

"And to think, for that we have to thank the contractors!"

---

*By the work one knows the workman.*

—J. DE LA FONTAINE

# 8

# how much is that router in the window?

...

*Wherever two or more male homeowners are gathered, they start rhapsodizing romantically about routers, drills, and scroll saws. Boys sure love their toys.*

My husband is lusting again.

Over a buddy's table saw.

Just what is it with men and their tools? Whenever two or more guys get together, they rhapsodize about their power tools. "I have a seven-hundred-dollar rechargeable megadrill that can drill through anything in less than three seconds and hold a charge for seventy-two hours, *and* it comes in its own carrying case," one guy announces.

His buddy starts salivating, asks if it's available at Home Depot, then tells his wife he has to make a quick run to the hardware store.

What I want to know is, why is it that whenever a guy starts a new yard or home-improvement project, it always seems to require the purchase of new power tools?

The last project around our house necessitated something called a Sawzall (it saws through it all) and yet *another* cordless drill gun.

"Why do you need another drill gun?" I asked Michael.

"Because," my beloved replied in that all-too-patient tone, "one is to drill the pilot hole, and the other is to screw in the screw. It would take too long to keep swapping out the bits."

Oh well. It was cheaper than hiring a contractor to do the job.

Then there are the tools he's purchased but never even used. "Hey, I got them at a yard sale. They were a bargain."

Our friends Lonnie and Joe moved into their red brick, pre–Civil War, two-story rural Michigan farmhouse as renters with the stipulation that as soon as they got a mortgage and a down payment, they'd buy the place.

"The house had a nice, big patio, so I wanted to get a set of wicker furniture to use outdoors," Lonnie recalled. "Four nice pieces of wicker on sale for just $199. And to this idea, my husband, Joe, calmly said, 'I have two words for you: down payment.'"

So Lonnie nixed the idea of her wicker set for the greater good.

A couple weeks later, Joe found a new tool for the house and came home to tell his sweet wife about it before buying it.

"How much?" Lonnie asked.

"About two hundred dollars," Joe replied.

"I have two words for you: down payment," she said. Joe thought for a minute and said, "Buy the wicker." He got his gadget guilt free.

But my brother-in-law Bob really takes the toolbox cake. Lately he's been making a lot of outdoor improvements to his yard, and recently at a family barbecue he announced with that glazed, tool-lust gleam in his eyes, "I'm going to plant hedges so I can go buy this really great hedge trimmer I saw at the hardware store!"

Ah, men and their toys. I mean, *tools*.

Barb says her husband, Frank, a mechanical contractor (heating/air-conditioning, electrical, sheet metal, etc.) has to be in on any activity that involves any home-improvement project. "He winds up doing a lot of the work himself," my cousin said. "Sometimes the general contractor would do something during the day, and Frank would take it apart at night and redo it—the right way. Of course, this meant buying a lot of new tools and more of those that we already had six of because he couldn't remember where he'd laid them. Our garage could pass for a Home Depot."

My pal Katie has learned an important tool lesson: "If someone who lives with you, like your husband, is going to work on a home-improvement project, it's going to require a tool, and it will *not* be on sale because Home Depot knows you need it."

Ralph and Maria, my city slicker friends who bought a 1920s farmhouse in the South Dakota countryside, quickly learned well enough how to do a lot of home-improvement things. However, they were both feeling very inept at driving in nails. "We knew oak was tough, and we drilled holes first to make it easier—just like the book said," Maria recalled. "But we always seemed to bend the nails before they fully sunk in. My father and mother visited us in the summer, and we found out why. Dad laughed and said, 'You're using a roofing hammer. You need a carpentry hammer.'

"That was another notch in my respect for people in the trade," Maria said. "You mean there's more than one type of hammer?"

They got the nails in straight after that.

"Tools are everything," Maria insists.

Although she says that "measure twice and cut once" rule is even better. "I tended to like the measure twice part,"

**Tools are everything.**

she said, "but Ralph always seemed to like to measure three or four times and to cut boards a little conservatively—just to make sure. His surgery training, no doubt, but remember, I'm the little woman holding up some pretty hefty pieces of wood while he cuts, putting them on sawhorses, and carrying them in and out of the house with him. Let's just say our approach to things was a little different.

"We bought every bit of tools, machinery, measuring pieces, etc., known to humans and packed in a store," Maria added. "We had to, since we discovered that tools were everything. In fact, we considered it cheaper than getting a divorce, which is what we could imagine doing if we had to redo everything over and over again like those first nails."

My single girlfriend Kim said her dad was on power-tool probation after a couple home-improvement fiascos but was still allowed to do handiwork around the house. So he decided he would put up the shelves in her bedroom.

The first two were little trouble, mostly getting things level. The last and biggest shelf wasn't so easy.

After marking off the spots on the wall for the nails, he nailed in one set while Kim was watching TV at the other end of the house—trying to drown out the pounding. When her dad started to nail in the other bracket, he discovered the nail wouldn't go into the stud. He thought he'd hit a knot or just a really hard spot in the wood. So after failing to put a couple regular nails into the hard area, he went and got a cement nail, thinking, *This will go into* any*thing.*

He slammed the nail home, and *thwack*. At the same instant, the TV went off. "Dad, what did you do?"

Turns out he'd put a cement nail through the wall into the electrical box on the outside of the house—nailing through the metal that's supposed to protect the box.

When the real handyman showed up to fix things, he opened the box and found a singed area. "My dad had managed to hit the smallest confined area, where there was very little oxygen, so a fire didn't have a chance," Kim recalled. "In addition, he was holding a rubber-handled hammer and wearing tennis shoes. The handyman said we were very lucky.

"The good thing is that Dad's okay. The bad thing is that I can never take down the shelf because of the nasty scar under the one bracket leg."

Kim said her dad was confined to working outside the house after this incident.

Kim recalls that one day he was nailing little knickknacky things on the garage walls. "Although why you need knick-knacks on the garage walls I don't know," my less-is-more friend said. All of a sudden, he heard a slight hiss. He suddenly realized he'd nailed into a water pipe and started a leak. He turned off the water and hollered to his wife, Nicki, to fill the tubs and sinks with whatever water was in the pipes because no more would be coming for a while.

Yet before I could think her dad was a total home-improvement failure, Kim hastened to add that he just finished installing a wood floor and it looks great.

"I think he only needed ten Band-Aids during the construction."

As a single woman and a homeowner, Jan started buying her own tools.

"Who needs men?" she said. She got a fancy red toolbox and filled it with a drill, staple gun—"Every woman needs one," she insisted—and all the things she'd need to be on call for her less fix-it inclined girlfriends. On the weekends, she attended a variety of home-improvement classes at Home Depot. As a result, Jan was able to fix her best friend Jeanne's swamp cooler and porch light, retexture the walls in her own bedroom, and put in a complete drip sprinkler system. (Hey, Jan, we're having trouble with our sprinklers—are you free next weekend?)

When Carl married Jan, he merged her tools with his. "After a few years, I started grumbling—which comes naturally for me—because I could never find a Phillips screwdriver when I needed one," Jan recalled. "It was always in his toolbox in his truck."

To keep his handywoman wife happy, for her birthday that year Carl bought her a brand-new red toolbox and outfitted it with everything she'd need.

My cousin Debbie, wanting to do something similarly nice for her husband, Roy, early in their marriage, went out and cleaned the garage for him. Now what you have to understand is that Debbie, like me, is a daughter of one of "the Miller girls." And all the Miller girls (both our moms and all their sisters) have a peculiar trait in common.

The cleanliness trait.

Those women are the world's best housekeepers. Everything in their homes has to be absolutely spotless. You've heard the saying "That floor's so clean you could eat off it"? Well, in a Miller girl's home, you could substitute bathtub, garage, or even toilet for the word *floor* and it wouldn't be a stretch.

So as a good Miller descendant, Debbie went out and cleaned her husband's garage for him. "I scrubbed all his screwdrivers and tools and got all the grease and yucky stuff off," she told me proudly.

Roy flipped.

Debbie laughs now retelling the story. "Roy always tells people how I scrubbed all the oil off his tools—how I Pine-Sol'ed all his tools.

"At least they smelled good."

*Plans fail for lack of counsel, but with many advisers they succeed.*

—PROVERBS 15:22

# 9

## stop and smell the roses—just don't move the rosebush!

• • •

*His 'n' her landscaping differences.*

My best friend Lana and her husband, Michael, decided to have a swimming pool built in their California backyard. When they met with the pool guys, the couple learned they'd have to take down part of their fence so the workers could bring a backhoe into the yard.

Not a problem. That came later.

A couple years before, Lana, who's the gardener in the family, had planted a miniature rose bush in front of the fence, right in the center, and had lovingly tended and nurtured the roses so that they were now a thing of beauty as well as her pride and joy.

"You'll go around my rose bush with the hoe, right?" Lana asked the pool guys before they started.

The workers looked at Michael, who looked over at his wife and then back to the pool guys, and the three men all burst out laughing.

In the end, the roses were removed. "Isn't that just like a man?" Lana said. "They can't go *around* the bush; they have to go right through it."

When the backhoe began its heavy, inexorable push past where the rosebush once bloomed, it got stuck in the mud and couldn't move. The workers had to have another truck come and tow out the backhoe. And Michael had to invest in a large three-hundred-dollar metal plate to lay on the ground so the backhoe could drive across the mud and grass into the backyard.

Hmm. Sounds like a little floral justice if you ask me.

My Michael has a co-worker named Jennifer, who is engaged to Jay. One day, Jay decided to help his fiancée out by doing some yard work at her house. Wanting to surprise her, he dug up the whole front yard and planted annuals. When Jennifer got home, Jay pointed proudly to his floral handiwork and said, "How do you like it?"

Problem was, he'd dug up all the bulbs she'd been working on for years.

Then there's Jan's husband, Carl.

Carl's a pruner. He likes to trim back and shape any and all kinds of greenery. "Before we got married, he bought me a pruner—one of those long poles with a saw on the end,"

Jan recalled. Then her smitten fiancé helpfully offered to prune Jan's mulberry trees for her. "I came out an hour later, and he had butchered my tree and cut away the limbs that shaded the entire deck," she said.

The soon-to-be-bride took one look and began to cry.

"Carl looked at me in horror, as I had portrayed myself to be an even-keeled and easygoing woman," Jan said. After her tears dried, she realized it was simply that her intended didn't understand the flow of her yard and went a little wacky with his trusty pruner.

"We got married anyway," she said.

The next year Carl told his beloved he was going to just "snip a bit" in the yard. "He's the snipper; I'm the planter and design genius," Jan explained. During their first year of wedded bliss, Jan had forgotten all about the premarital mulberry tree incident and her sweetheart's penchant for pruning and paring. This time when she went outside, she discovered her husband had desecrated her apricot tree—in the fall, when the leaves were still on the tree.

"Carl, honey . . . darling . . . fruit trees must be pruned in winter when they are dormant," she lovingly explained to her green-thumb-impaired husband.

"Oops. Sorry."

Jan didn't cry—yet. Not until the next year when she didn't get a single apricot from her fruit tree. "You stressed my tree!" she told her other half. "I'm repossessing your pruner."

> **"He's 'neatening up,' so he thinks. I say he's just addicted to the click of the shears."**

Carl is still hopeless, Jan says. "I find him sneaking around snipping and slashing whenever he gets a chance. He's 'neat-

103

ening up,' so he thinks. I say he's just addicted to the click of the shears."

For Carl, it's a form and fashion fetish. "I just love the open look, don't you?" he'll ask his wife as he stands and proudly surveys his creations.

"We have no blooming trees in our yard anymore, but he's happy," Jan said. "And the fruit tree is too confused to produce. Now I just buy my apricots."

But let's not be sexist here. It's not just men who prune and pillage green growing things.

One day my impulsive friend Andrea decided she didn't like the sixty-year-old camellia tree that was covering the front windows of her lovely "new" home, so she determined to trim it back.

She sought out her husband, Bill, who was downstairs taking one of his "coma" naps, and asked, "Honey, do we have a clippers?"

A subconscious "mm-hmm" was her dead-to-the-world husband's reply, so Andrea took matters into her own hands. She found the clippers, then advanced to loppers, and finally progressed to the shovel; whereupon she stood on the shovel, leaned back, broke the handle off, and fell on her backside.

Back downstairs to her still dead-to-the-world husband with another request.

"Honey, do we have another shovel?"

The soundly napping Bill never moved his lips. He simply said "mm-hmm" again.

Andrea tried once more and got yet another non-lip-moving, informative "mm-hmm."

*Fine. Whatever,* his wife thought. *I can do this. I'll surprise him. When he awakes, the tree will be out.*

So Andrea searched through her husband's tools, found an ax, and got as far as she could with it, but finally frustrated, she went back inside and asked Bill if he could please help.

Her exhausted, still coma-napping husband emitted another "mm-hmm."

"Charged by anger and home-improvement abandon, I went back outside, climbed up the tree, and broke off the limbs by, believe it or not, jumping up and down on them until I got down to the nubs," my industrious girlfriend recalled.

Finally Andrea was faced with just the stump of the beautiful sixty-year-old camellia tree, and in the meantime, the neighbors had gathered to stand around and watch. "I was feeling pressure to perform. I was new in the neighborhood," she said. "Problem was, I was out of fuel, exhausted, scratched up, and clearly out of 'new tool' ideas."

Covered in spiderwebs, leaves, and dirt, Andrea returned downstairs one final time to ask Bill if they had a chain saw and a "wench" (winch) that she could hook to the truck to pull the stump out. "I got another one of those comatose, fact-filled 'mm-hmm' responses," my friend said. "Defeated, I was going to either submit to this stump or rethink my strategy."

In this instance, by the time Andrea got back outside to curse the camellia gods, Mr. Coma Man came flying out the front door, eyes swollen with sleep, bed-head hair and all, to the sight of the sixty-year-old tree now reduced to a pile bigger than their Nissan truck.

This time Bill was spouting more than non-lip-moving dialogue. Way more. "Let's just say he helped me finish the project—a bit dumbfounded," Andrea said.

105

When it comes to trees, Michael is a complete 180 from both Andrea and Carl. Even though we live in California, my husband is not your basic tree hugger. He simply loves trees—particularly all the ones in our yard, which is one of the main reasons we bought our house.

He and I both mourned the day our tall, fifty-year-old Modesto ash, which provided glorious shade and coolness to the front of our house, was cut down. Granted, we knew the tree was diseased and dying—the mistletoe we had to have removed every year was proof of that. So when a local tree expert in conjunction with the county worked out a deal to cut down all the dying and diseased trees in the neighborhood (all the same type of tree and planted fifty years earlier when the neighborhood was created), we reluctantly agreed. Problem was, we'd never been informed exactly when they were going to remove ours. We'd been out of town for a three-day weekend, and when we arrived home Monday morning, we pulled up to our house just as the tree came crashing down into the street.

It was a heartbreaking sight.

Which is why when we did a major backyard renovation that included hiring workers to build a garden shed, we weren't about to lose any more trees.

For years, Michael and I had been talking about installing a pretty storage shed in a shady, ivy-covered section way in the back of the yard which we always referred to as "the secret garden." But it wasn't until my car, which we always kept parked in the driveway, was broken into that the shed became a necessity. We needed someplace to store everything we had crammed in the garage so my car could fit there instead.

We started shed shopping and found a couple we liked that were also reasonably priced. My sweetie and I didn't want plastic or metal—we preferred a charming wooden shed that would look like a miniature cottage on the outside but would provide functional storage inside. The kicker was that for the reasonably priced wood ones, you had to install the entire thing yourself, from pouring the cement slab to building it from the ground up and painting. We didn't have the time or physical stamina to do that. (Although I can wield a hammer pretty efficiently, it's mostly for the indoor picture-hanging realm.)

Instead, we decided that since we'd recently received a larger-than-expected check in the mail, we'd go for broke and order a shed from one of those specialty places where we could decide exactly what we wanted and the company would send a couple workers to build our shed from the ground up.

In four hours, no less.

Yes, it was more expensive than the kits you build yourself, but it was still half the cost of the custom-made shed in my girlfriend's backyard, so we felt it was a good deal.

Since it was only supposed to take about four or five hours max to install the shed, Michael took the morning off work to be home while the guys were building the shed.

The workers arrived at 9:00 a.m. Pretty quickly, however, it was determined that the 8 x 12 shed wouldn't fit into the place we'd measured out, even though a former twelve-foot structure that served as a pigeon coop used to sit on the same spot. We hadn't been told to take into account the extra few inches necessary for the overhanging roof. So now the shed needed to be angled to fit into the space.

No problem. That's what I'd wanted in the first place.

The builders started to work, but once they had the rear and right walls of the building constructed, they realized that the left wall would hit a lovely old cherry tree that provided more than a third of the shade for our secret garden. One of the workers wanted to cut a chunk out of the tree trunk to ensure that the shed would fit, but my nature-loving husband wouldn't have any of that.

Michael came up with a better idea: "Can't we just move the partial shed before it's completely built instead?"

But the builders informed him that it would take six or seven guys to move the shed at that point. The one worker again suggested cutting into the tree trunk to make it work, and Michael again demurred, not wanting to damage the tree in any way. Finally, after the third time, my husband reluctantly agreed, but only if there was no other option.

By this time, however, it had already been more than four and a half hours, and the shed was still far from being done. And Michael had to go to work.

A couple hours later when I went to check on the progress of the shed, it was nearly complete and looked wonderful, even in its unfinished state. Already I could envision it painted blue and white and looking all darling and cottagey.

But then I noticed the cherry tree crunching into the rooftop and bending the metal trim.

"Oh, we told your husband that would be a problem, but he told us to just go ahead and keep building," the guys reassured me.

*Really?*

Now it was my turn to ask if the shed could be moved farther away from the tree.

108

"No way," one of the guys said. "It would take maybe eight to ten guys to move that whole thing at this point. Can't be done. You're just going to have to cut that tree down."

I explained that my husband loved the tree and that we'd planned our whole garden around the fact that it was a shade garden. If we lost the tree, we'd lose nearly half the shade and the privacy it created. So that wasn't a viable solution.

The other builder came up with another option: "You can probably pull the tree back away from the shed with some heavy-duty cables or wires and stake them to the ground—my parents did that in their yard. Otherwise, you can probably just cut the one branch and it should be fine."

What a relief. That prospect sounded very doable to me, a novice when it came to green growing things.

When Michael returned home that night and saw the way the shed was jammed up tightly against the tree, he wasn't happy. I mentioned the guy's suggestion to simply cut the one branch off, but my more nature savvy husband explained that the "branch" was actually a tree trunk—one of three growing out from the base of the tree.

Oh.

A couple days later, after repeated calls to the shed company to complain, the owner contacted us, apologized for the delay and offered to have an arborist friend come out, assess the situation, and give us the benefit of his expertise.

Relieved, we agreed, looking forward to resolving the issue.

The next day when the shed owner and his arborist buddy arrived (again, while Michael was at work) the arborist took one look at the shed and the tree and announced that the only solution was to cut down the whole tree.

"But what about pulling it back with wires and cables like the one guy said?" I asked.

"Doesn't work with mature trees. Nope. The only solution is to chop down the tree, and I can do that for you, no problem. You've got a nice new shed here; you don't want to mess it up." He looked around the rest of our secret garden and backyard and announced that we should also get rid of some other trees, which again, he'd be happy to do for us. For a fee.

I'd always thought arborists were tree lovers. Guess not. At least not this guy. He seemed to be itching to chop down or cut back all our trees and greenery. The decades-old trees and greenery we loved and that provided our backyard with shade and privacy.

We passed.

So now we have our adorable blue-and-white garden shed complete with flowering window boxes and hanging plants—with our mature cherry tree joined to the roof.

Ken, our Herculean handyman friend married to the lucky Pat, built a gorgeous white Victorian gazebo in their backyard, complete with lovely scrollwork, piped-in music, and misters for the hanging plants. The couple had originally ordered some gazebo plans from a gardening magazine, but it wasn't exactly what they wanted, so talented, problem-solving Ken adapted them to fit his needs.

"I make it up as I go," he said.

Prior to beginning construction, Ken went out and stood in the yard for about half an hour figuring out the best way to begin. *Let's see. I want an eight-sided circular gazebo, so I'd take 360 degrees and divide by eight, which gives me 45 degrees.*

*Then divide that by two to get the angle for each rail cut, which would work out to 22 ½.*

As Ken recounted his calculations over dinner with us one night, Michael listened in rapt fascination, but my head began to hurt.

"You just *knew* that?" I asked Ken, amazed.

"Knew what?"

"That there's 360 degrees in a circle."

Ken shot an incredulous look at Michael. "That's pretty basic, Laura."

Not for those of us who hate math.

Ken also built—alone and from scratch—a darling Victorian garden-cum-potting shed for Pat that looks like an oversized dollhouse in shades of pink, rose, and dusty blue, complete with gables and gingerbread trim.

Prior to construction when her husband was planning things out, Pat told him, "I'll need water and a sink inside, because I'm going to pot plants in there."

"No you're not," Ken said. "You just like the *idea* of being able to do that, but you'll never do it." (She always sat outside at their old picnic table to do her potting.)

"Yes I will," Pat insisted.

But after thirty years of marriage, Ken knew his wife well enough to know that reality was different than her fantasies, and he wasn't about to pipe in water for something she might use only once.

Pat reluctantly agreed that her husband was right. In all the years she's had that pretty garden shed, she's only potted one plant in there. "But if I'd had the sink," she said, smiling slyly at him over our dinner table, "I might have done more."

I hear that. You go, Pat.

111

When my friend Lori and her husband, "Tim," bought their last house, it was on a large lot, and they decided they needed to have a deck in the front yard instead of a porch. The couple didn't have much money for the project, so they had to window shop and calculate how much it would cost and then save up.

In the meantime, Tim dug all the post holes so they would be ready when they brought the supplies home. But when they got home from work each day, somehow, mysteriously, the holes would be filled back in with dirt! "This went on for days," Lori recalled. "We would have videotaped it so we could find out what was going on, but we didn't have a recorder and couldn't afford one, so the problem continued. Our kids finally caught on. Seems the neighbor kids thought it was all a big game, and they were stopping by on their way home from school each day and filling in the holes."

Finally the big day came when Lori and Tim made the trek to the home-improvement store to bring home all the deck-building supplies. By the time they got home, however, it was dark and too late to start, so they left the wood piled up in the front yard, ready for an early start the next morning.

Unfortunately, it rained all night and warped all their brand-new wood.

Since the couple couldn't afford more wood, they tried to make do with the bent wood they had. Lori's job was to hold the little nail they used as a spacer in between the planks of wood so they would all be equal distance apart. They started at one end, where Tim screwed the plank down, then moved to the other end, where Lori once again held the nail in just the right place for her husband. "The problem was that with the warped wood, Tim would have to kick the wood over tight and then screw it down fast," Lori recalled. "With my delicate little fingers in this dangerous spot (a fact that I didn't catch on to right away), my husband would heave his entire six-foot-two, 280-pound frame onto the piece of wood, which would promptly jump its rail and smash my fingers. After yelling at me for deserting my post, we'd try it again." After that piece was successfully screwed down, Tim would hand Lori another nail (hers had dropped below the deck level), smile, and say, "Ready for another one?"

"Whenever he mentioned the deck, I would break out in tears," Lori recalled. "The neighbors were so amused that they would bring out their lawn chairs and sit and watch us. We were the entertainment for the entire neighborhood.

"By the time it was over," Lori said, "I had no fingers left, we weren't speaking, and we later discovered that we had buried some of our tools underneath the deck surface. They're still there to this day."

Lori's vowed never to build a deck with a man again.

My friend Judi is a great bargain hunter, and a while back at an outdoor market she was thrilled to find a large—we're talking really large, say maybe four feet high—clay flowerpot that sold at a local nursery for twice the price. She loved the pot, which was decorated with three-dimensional lemons and was perfect for the empty corner in their backyard.

When she returned home from the market with her outdoor find towering in the back of her Ford Explorer, her husband, Jim, took one look at the huge—and insanely heavy—clay pot and said, "You've gotta be kidding!"

Although it had taken four strong men at the outdoor market to load it into the Explorer, Judi hadn't given a thought as to how she'd get the pot out of the vehicle once she got home. She was just so excited by the great bargain that she threw every other practical thought out of her pretty little head.

Her husband's head was far more practical. "The backyard? You want this carried to the backyard?"

Judi quickly enlisted the help of their grown son and Bob, the next door neighbor, for the necessary he-man strength. (One less than the number of guys at the market, if you'll recall.)

The men put their heads together, then their muscles, and slid the pot down a piece of foam padding into an old wheelbarrow. While her husband pushed, the other two guys carefully balanced the terra cotta monstrosity. They made it three steps before the wheel collapsed and the weight of the pot flattened the rim of the wheelbarrow.

Judi stepped in to help by putting her weight on the wheelbarrow handles as the guys tipped the nose of it low enough to roll the clay pot out.

Roll? It rolls!

"Let's roll it the rest of the way!" neighbor Bob suggested. As Jim and Bob rotated the rim of the pot while her son supervised, Judi watched her 3D lemons being sanded away on the concrete.

Oops.

Then the guys came up with a new remedy: set the pot on a rug and slide it the rest of the way. Except the rug had a rubber backing, which made sliding difficult. Next came a large piece of cardboard, which worked like a charm until it was pulled off the rug.

So for the last few feet, Judi's husband and son pulled while the neighbor ran in circles moving the rug from back to front.

Finally they reached the appointed destination, and the three men used up their last vestiges of strength and heaved the pot onto its final resting place in the corner of the backyard. Judi started to ask if they could turn the flattened lemons toward the back, but her husband's "never again" mutter effectively silenced her.

Besides, her daughter-in-law says the scratches and flat lemons add character.

Judi loves her pot, flaws and all. Although recently she noticed that it's crowding two bay trees. She wonders how long she should wait before suggesting to her husband that they move the trees.

That would be *forever* if she were married to my Michael.

---

*Flowers . . . are a proud assertion that a ray of beauty outvalues all the utilities of the world.*

—RALPH WALDO EMERSON

115

# 10

# home not-so-sweet home improvement, part two

...

*More tales from the remodeling netherworld.*

Six years ago, my Texas cousin Debbie and her husband, Roy, bought three and a half acres of land in the countryside about an hour south of Dallas where they planned to build their dream house. The property was part of an old ranch that the original owners had decided to break up and sell in minimums of three-acre lots, and the only hint of civilization was the road into the cul-de-sac where Debbie and Roy's new house would be located.

Initially my cousin thought she'd like a "new" two-story Victorian, but when she and Roy realized this would—hopefully—be the last house they ever owned, neither of them wanted to have to climb stairs in their old age, so they opted to build a beautiful one-story planter-style house instead.

But the building was still quite a ways off. First they had to clear their heavily wooded land.

Although they'd hoped to hire manual laborers for the thankless task, the only workers they could find who were willing to do that kind of heavy manual labor were Hispanic laborers who didn't speak any English. My cousins spoke very little Spanish, but Debbie did learn the word for "cut." Only problem was, the workers interpreted it to mean cut *everything* down.

Can you say failure to communicate?

"Our land would have ended up a desert," Debbie said. Since my cousins wanted to be "real picky about which trees got cut and which ones didn't," they wound up clearing the land themselves—with a little help from their friends.

They went out every Sunday and cut trees and cleared underbrush for what would eventually become a 120-square-foot clearing for the house and front turf area. "It was just like being a pioneer woman," Debbie recalled of those countless weekends spent chopping and cutting. "No pretty fingernails anymore." You'd have to know my beautiful and always impeccably made-up cousin to know what a major 180 this was for her. Not to mention that she's a native Texan, and I hear that in Texas womanly beauty is an art form and big hair and the proper way to accessorize are courses taught in college.

Additionally, there were no nearby facilities for answering the call of Mother Nature—just them, their truck, and the land—so Debbie and her girlfriends would have to "Girl Scout" it to go to the bathroom. The guys, of course, did their Boy Scout thing too, but it was a little easier on them than on the women. "We kept an emergency kit at the back of the truck with toilet paper and other essentials the girls would need, as well as insecticide to spray our bodies down," Debbie said.

The land clearing was a slow, laborious process. "We decided we should own stock in chain saws, because we bought so many," Debbie said. "You can only use those blades so long and then they die." The couple also bought a tractor, to which they hooked up chains to pull down trees. "We could never have done it without a tractor."

> **"We decided we should own stock in chain saws, because we bought so many."**

Since Roy and Debbie maintained full work schedules at the busy photography studio they owned in the city, they had to squeeze in work on their country property on the weekends—around inclement weather and family and professional obligations.

Finally, two and a half years after they cut down their first tree, the land was cleared and ready for the foundation to be poured.

Unfortunately, the house was initially bid at fourteen thousand dollars for the foundation, but the cost skyrocketed to forty-six thousand because their dream was to be positioned at the top of the hill and the original bid didn't allow for a six-and-a-half foot drop from one corner to the other.

As a result, they had to bring in about sixteen thousand dollars worth of additional dirt. "Just dirt!" Debbie said. Once everything was leveled, the structural engineer informed the couple that they'd need to drop sixty-one concrete rebarb piers at eighteen inches round by fifteen feet deep, which took four days of drilling. Then, on their scheduled "pour day," the concrete trucks started arriving, but the pump truck, which takes the concrete from the concrete truck and pumps it into the foundation, was detained because the driver didn't have the proper permit for their country roads.

So they had to reschedule and start again.

Once the foundation was complete, the couple had an incredible piece of concrete on top of a hill with a gorgeous view of the surrounding countryside. Roy said to his wife, "Okay, Deb, we're just going to back up a double-wide and set it on the foundation, because if all the other prices keep increasing this same way, we won't be able to afford to build the house. We can't take any more hits."

"It was a real *Money Pit* situation," Debbie recalled.

Thankfully, they didn't encounter any other major home-building increases over the next year while their house was being built. Although they ran into one or two occasions where the construction cost exceeded the bid, they didn't let that stop them from forging ahead with the building of their dream home. Sometimes, though, it meant Roy and a friend took on the job themselves to cut expenses—which meant the forging had to take a little longer. "We kept adjusting our priority/dream list to accommodate the budget increases," Debbie recalled.

A year later, their beautiful three-thousand-square-foot, four-bedroom, three-bath dream home on a hill was completed.

And the first time I caught sight of it, I thought I'd died and gone to Tara.

The only thing missing was Scarlett sipping a mint julep on the veranda while surrounded by a throng of admirers.

Debbie gently corrected my Yankee girl mistake. "Ours is more like the smaller house next to the big plantation—where the overseer might live. It has square columns rather than round, and the porch, open main floor plan, sloped ceilings, and French-style windows make it more planter style."

Planter, plantation. Whatever you call it, their new house looked drop-dead gorgeous to me. I fell head over heels for the fabulous front porch with a lovely swing on either end. (The swings are Debbie's favorite part.) My cousin said they specifically designed the porch to be fifty-two feet long and ten feet deep so they could eat outside comfortably—no squeezing into a table and chairs—and kick back and relax with ease.

Roy hired an artist to create an eight-foot-long sign for the porch with this quotation by John Haskins: "I have long been convinced that any of mankind's problems could be properly brought to bay on a good front porch."

Although their pretty porch seduced me with its southern charm (and I agree with Debbie when she says, "A lot of problem solving can get done on a good porch with a good breeze"), I have to confess that once we stepped inside, it was the kitchen that claimed a permanent hold on my heart. A gleaming island in the center, *two* sinks—one facing the backyard with its bevy of abundant flowers and lovely landscaping, and the other directly opposite and facing the great room where Debbie, or whoever was cooking, could chat easily with guests—plus a curved eating bar on the other side of that sink with tall, white bar stools I wanted to take home in my luggage.

And loads and loads of cupboard space.

Serious kitchen envy happening on my end now.

But it was the tribute-to-the-fifties soda fountain booth in the far corner that really captivated me—complete with red-checked cushions, an old-fashioned pop-up straw dispenser, and fun reproduction Coca-Cola signs coupled with other American memorabilia. Debbie had always wanted a nostalgic booth, so her handyman knight built it for her. And the two of them enjoy the occasional romantic milk shake with two straws in the cozy seats. Although recently the grandkids have taken it over.

Our friends Bill and Andrea bought a darling two-bedroom 1940s fixer-upper cottage late one summer and moved in thinking, *We'll be done with this remodel in no time.*

"I thought we'd be done in six months—definitely by Christmas," Andrea recalled. "But Bill said I use a different calendar than the rest of society."

But what the couple hadn't realized was exactly how much work the house actually needed and how

> **"I thought we'd be done in six months—definitely by Christmas," Andrea recalled. "But Bill said I use a different calendar than the rest of society."**

time-consuming it would all turn out to be. Rather than tackling the renovation room by room, they tried to do everything all at once. They had to completely gut the kitchen and the powder room. Every single room in the house was replastered and every ceiling Sheetrocked and replastered by "I can fix anything" hubby. Plus all new baseboards, window trim, crown molding—the works. "Bill replastered the walls back to the original time period, since someone had come in and done that funky sixties texturing," Andrea said.

121

The couple hired someone to install French doors to the backyard where two bedroom windows once lived. Bill created arches where doors once stood, installed a slate floor in the kitchen, installed retro tile in the bathroom, and installed hardwood floors in the laundry room and powder room.

He hired someone to do the electrical and had new heat and air professionally installed due to an old asbestos-filled heater. "When we had the old heater checked, the guy told us we'd be fine keeping it as long as we didn't have babies or old people breathing the air," Andrea recalled. "Money was tight, so I looked at our address book to see who to exclude. But Bill did the right thing and had it removed.

"There went my new sofa."

For six months, Bill and Andrea didn't have a kitchen, and for three months, their new toilet sat in the middle of the kitchen while the bathroom was being remodeled.

For a month, the couple wound up showering at the gym since their shower was gutted. "You don't get a plumber on demand," Andrea informed me. "It took weeks to fix. On the weekends we'd come into the gym at 5:50 looking like we were homeless after working on the house all day," she recalled, "and the perky little receptionist with her perfect white teeth and not a hair out of place would look at us and say, 'We close at six.'"

At one point in the remodeling process, the couple also found dry rot and learned that the flue in the fireplace wasn't working. "We didn't get extended warranties or insurance, because I thought, *I'm married to Bill. Bill can fix it*," Andrea said.

Another time, they slept in the basement on an inflatable bed for a couple weeks while they had their hardwood floors refinished. "Two cats, one border collie, and us," Andrea recalled.

My interior-design-conscious friend, who's an executive at an upscale department store, has a keen decorating sense. "I would sit and dream, *Wouldn't it be great if we did* . . . Then I'd point, shoot, pick out the colors, and leave, because Bill knew that 'we' meant him. I used my carpal tunnel to the nth degree," Andrea confessed.

Always on top of the latest trends, one day she bought a Home Depot chandelier for the dining room, added crystal prisms, and topped the lights with leopard-print shades.

Bill took one look at the animal design, raised his eyebrows, and said to his wife, "Is it going to take long for you to work through this stage, Zsa Zsa?"

> **Bill took one look at the animal design, raised his eyebrows, and said to his wife, "Is it going to take long for you to work through this stage, Zsa Zsa?"**

Johnny and Jeannie bought their large, three-story Queen Anne Victorian five years ago. It started out as a single family home but in 1920 became a duplex. Over the years, the middle floor of the three-story house has been many businesses, including an attorney's office.

"We made an offer on it the first day we saw the inside," Jeannie recalled. "It had been on the market a week, but no one had been able to get inside. We were part of a group that met to go inside, and we knew as soon as we stepped through the front door that it had great potential." The couple had been looking for two years for a home downtown, ever since they felt the call to plant a church in the city's urban area. "Our biggest challenge was finding a home where my mother-in-law, Norma, could have her own space that was more than just a bedroom," Jeannie said.

When Johnny looked at the "disastrous" basement, which was ground level, he had the vision and foresight to see it as a beautiful apartment for his mom. It already had above-ground windows all around, but it also had a six-foot ceiling, no plumbing, "scary electrical wiring," a rotten floor, and a host of other problems.

"I was skeptical, and I think Norma was too," Jeannie recalled, "but she had more faith than I did. We were all driven by the potential of this separate space, and we saw that the floor plan of the other two floors could work with some adjustments, so we made an offer that day, pending our contractor friend giving a good inspection.

"Everyone else in the group made offers that day too," Jeannie said, "but God had chosen the house for us, and we got it."

The family, including Johnny's mom, moved in to their "new" house sixty days later, and after almost a year, Norma's basement apartment was ready for her to make her home.

Jeannie and Johnny hadn't planned on changing the house's original brick foundation, but after inspections and committing to remodel the basement, they were encouraged to take the bricks out and have a cement foundation poured. "It would have been a huge risk to put in a new floor without moving the foundation," Johnny said. Once the original brick foundation was knocked out, the family was sitting on air, or rather heavy jacks, for three months as work commenced. "You could see completely underneath the house all the way to the backyard," Jeannie recalled. They also lived with steel beams sticking out of the windows on each end of the house to help brace it, as well as two-by-fours in the living room.

Johnny explained that the workers had to do "reverse building," pouring the cement up to the existing jack level below the house. Normally, the foundation of a house is poured first and then the house built atop it. But in this situation, the 120-year-old house was already built, and they needed to pour the foundation beneath it.

To the tune of an extra thirty thousand dollars the couple hadn't planned on.

"The house probably could have sat on this foundation for another hundred years, but in the process of remodeling the basement, it was a natural, although expensive, time to change the brick foundation," Jeannie said.

"The mortar in between the bricks was like dust," she recalled. The bricks were saved, and over the next year Norma cleaned off old bits of cement and separated the ones stuck together, and now they have a lovely brick path circling the house. Another stack is waiting to make a small sitting area in the front yard and a patio for the backyard. "Norma sat on a stool and used a little hammer to clean every single brick," Jeannie said.

"She'd clean them, and I'd lay them," Johnny said.

"As she worked on the bricks, she would visit with all the neighbors as they walked by," Jeannie said, "and they would tease her about us demanding 'hard labor' and that she should be wearing a prison suit. It was very satisfying work for her, though, and she made a great contribution to preserving our original bricks."

Jeannie and Johnny adore their drop-dead gorgeous Victorian, which they've since learned is one of a kind in town, with its specific architecture. It's considered one of the "jewels of the neighborhood"—something they didn't know when they bought it.

Their magnificent home has been lovingly restored and repainted in a pretty sea foam green (that looks almost robin's egg blue in some lights) with rose and buttercream trim and cream gingerbread accents.

Since moving in, they've met people who are purists about restoration and will go to great lengths and expense to track down antique, original light fixtures to go with their Victorians. But Jeannie and Johnny have neither the time nor the money to do so. Instead, they've installed reproduction light fixtures that closely resemble the original lighting. "We tried to get the nicest look possible," Jeannie said.

From my humble vantage point, they've succeeded admirably.

The couple has made many friends in the neighborhood, and their neighbors tell them they're happy that the jewel of the neighborhood was turned back into a single family dwelling. "We entertain neighbors all the time," Jeannie said. "Many of them have been remodeling their own homes for years. We are bonded on common ground and encourage one another."

Andrea, my *House Beautiful* friend, is in love with signs. "I have signs for everything," she says, "both inside and outside my house—in French. There's a sign on the bathroom door that says 'Toilettes,' another that says 'Bienvenue' (Welcome), another that says 'Mon Jardin' (My Garden), and another that says 'W/C' (Water Closet [another word for bathroom])."

Her patient, long-suffering husband, Bill, finally reached his sign limit and told Andrea, "No more signs!"

A couple weeks later, she came home with three more.

That's when Bill went to the catchall drawer, pulled out a packet of sticky notes, and started scribbling his own mini-signs to put up all over the house—"coffeemaker," "table," "sink," "husband." "He even put a sign on our border collie Jake's tail that said 'dog,'" Andrea recalled.

By the time her husband finished his handiwork, his wife was doubled over laughing, with tears streaming down her face.

"Okay, are you done with the signs now?" Bill said.

---

*Be content with what you have.*

---

—HEBREWS 13:5

127

# 11

# a room of his own

• • •

*Does the garage count? I get that he needs
his own space, but I don't see why he can't
decorate it in chintz and lace to go with
the rest of the house.*

In the first few weeks of our marriage, Michael and I were still in that blissful, wanting to do everything together state. Even boring household chores.

Doing dishes had never been so much fun. Nor had watching the spin cycle at the laundromat.

But then we made the bed together for the very first time.

And I was shocked to discover that my beloved had no idea how to make a bed. The bottom fitted sheet was no problem. Our pretty, floral, wedding-gift sheet was still so crisp and new that it automatically snapped into its proper place—and stayed.

The top sheet, however, was another story.

I took my side and lined it up carefully and methodically to the very top of the mattress. Michael pulled up his side, but stopped a good three inches from the top and then sauntered casually to the foot of the bed where he began to haphazardly tuck the sheet in any which way.

My linen sensibilities were appalled.

There were lumpy wrinkles in the sheet! Clearly, Michael had never served time with Uncle Sam.

In the service, you learn how to make proper military corners—also commonly referred to as "hospital corners." I learned during basic training at Lackland Air Force Base, Texas, in the mid-1970s. My mom and all her sisters learned how to make a taut bed from my Grandma Miller in the days when mothers still passed those domestic skills down to their daughters.

Michael never acquired those domestic skills, although he taught himself to sew years later when he decided he wanted to make a quilt of his own. Now *that's* a domestic art I've never mastered, nor do I want to—or even need to now, since I'm married to a man who sews.

But to sew and quilt and paint and work on the computer and tinker on myriad other projects, my husband needed a room of his own. Every man does—even those who don't sew. They all need a place to call their own without a woman's touch—or interference. Sorry, girls, but you know it's true.

> **My husband needed a room of his own. Every man does—even those who don't sew.**

So Michael has his room, a large portion of the garage, *and* his nice new garden shed.

I'm just grateful they all have doors that can be closed.

One thing my cousin Bettie was really looking forward to during their home remodel was her husband, Stacy, having his own shop downstairs. "I thought it was quite generous for us to plan out his having a room of his own," she recalled. "We'd talked about it over the years. And this was the solution to end our arguments about the garage always being in a state of disarray and never being able to find something when you needed it.

"I would cringe when that garage door was up and the neighbors could see in," she recalled. "Boy, I sure hoped they didn't think my house was as messy as that!"

Her husband having his own space would allow him to have benches, shelves, and cabinets. He'd need to pick up a few more tools, of course—a table saw, router, Shop-Vac, etc. But everything would have a place, neat and organized at last.

It's been over a year now, and not only does Bettie have a garage that she can barely tolerate parking her van in but now there's a dreaded room downstairs too. "I only venture in there when absolutely necessary," she said. "It's beyond a nightmare.

"What really gets me is that he still hasn't acquired all the things he needs to really make it a room he can enjoy putzing in," Bettie says. "At least I can be thankful that I had the sense to insist a door be built to close it off from the family room."

When Carl and Jan got married, he inherited the garage. "What a mess," he told his wife. "How did this happen?"

"Healthy neglect," she replied.

130

Carl went to work. First, he drywalled the garage and insulated the walls for comfort. It would be his retreat. Immediately he perched a TV on the wall so as not to miss his Fox News updates. "He bought a metal shed for 'my stuff,' and out to the side yard it went," Jan said. "That made room for my car, which had never experienced covered parking before. Now I have no claim on the garage whatsoever, except for laundry and my car. And he spent days trying to figure out how he could relocate the washer and dryer. He has systematized the entire garage," Jan said. "Everything has its place." Now he's installing cabinets over the washer and dryer to hide all his wife's cleaning supplies, which he encourages her to "consolidate" if possible.

"I can't stand the clutter," Carl said.

Works for Jan.

In Bill and Andrea's *House Beautiful* home, the den was supposed to be Bill's room, with its plaid wallpapered walls, leather furniture, and Ralph Lauren touches resembling an English country gentleman's estate. "Except Bill said he doesn't feel like he fits in there unless he's wearing suede slippers and a smoking jacket," Andrea said. "And for a Gap kind of man, that's never going to happen."

Roy, my cousin Debbie's photographer husband, doesn't have simply a room of his own, he has an entire building of his own—a huge 1,290-square-foot wood shop on the back of their three-and-a-half-acre property where he builds and designs cabinetry and handmade Windsor chairs. "That's supposed to be where his design input ends," Debbie said, "when he walks in the house. Decorating's supposed to be a girl's job, but he's got that artist's eye."

My cousin doesn't mind—most of the time—because Roy has excellent taste, but now and then she needs to exercise her feminine prerogative of what's typically the woman's domain—the inside of the house. "He has his territory, so go, get there, and do it," Debbie said.

Roy, don't take it personally. Confidentially, between you and me, I think it's more a matter of that genetic rearranging thing that runs in the female members of the Miller family.

At least Debbie doesn't come in and rearrange your workshop. Right?

---

*Everything will come if a man will only wait.*

---

—BENJAMIN DISRAELI

# 12

# the rearranging rumba

...

*Rearranging furniture is a girl thing. It's an
important, genetic rite of womanhood, but
men just don't seem to enjoy
the ritual dance.*

I'm a decorating diva. After writing, it's probably my
favorite creative outlet. Every time I finish another
book project, I immediately plunge into a frenzy of
housecleaning and redecorating—often with the help of
Lana, my best friend. Hey, I have a great idea! If my writing
juices ever dry up, maybe I can get a job on one of those
cable home-improvement shows where they surprise the
homeowner with a completely redecorated room.

Although I would never *ever* use orange as a wall or
window covering color. Trust me on this.

I absolutely love to decorate. Paint, wallpaper, swap one picture for another, display books in different groupings, use unusual items for things they weren't originally intended for. I once spray painted a fireplace insert red and used it as a magazine rack. And, of course, I love to rearrange the furniture.

Michael doesn't get it when I break into the rearranging rumba.

That's because it's a girl thing. I tell him the rearranging gene is an essential part of our female DNA. And I come from a long line of female furniture rearrangers—of whom my mom is the queen.

"I don't know why my sisters and I have always loved to rearrange furniture," Mom mused. "Maybe it was because my dad wouldn't let Mom or us kids do that when we were growing up." (All my mom's sisters have a penchant for the rearranging rumba, as their husbands will attest—sometimes while rubbing a bruised shin caused from bumping into a newly placed coffee table in the middle of the night.)

Mom started her rearranging career when she and my dad got married in the mid-1950s and all the relatives gave them odds and ends of used furniture for their first apartment. "It was fun to rearrange everything and give the room a whole new look with old cast-off furniture," Mom recalled. Someone had given them an old living room sofa, and then my Great Grandma Jensen asked Mom if they'd like this huge overstuffed sofa that Dad had always loved, so they had two sofas jammed into their very small living room.

"The only problem was that when your dad and his friends brought Grandma's sofa to our new upstairs flat, it was too big to get up the winding stairs, so they had to leave it on the front lawn," my mom recalled. My dad then had to call a moving company, and they lifted the sofa up with a crane and put it through the large window in the living room.

"It was a pretty free sofa, but we had to pay quite a bit to get it into the living room."

When I was really little, sometime around 1960 or 1961, we moved into a downstairs apartment in an older house. The kitchen had tall upper cabinets with glass doors, but because we had a conglomeration of mix-and-match dishes, Mom and Dad decided they didn't like the glass doors showing their hodge-podge of mismatched pieces. They decided instead to put pretty contact paper over the glass. "What a job that turned out to be," Mom recalled. As my dad and his buddy stuck on the contact paper, Mom and her girlfriend followed behind them with straight pins to prick all the tiny air bubbles that appeared.

But she says the end result was worth the effort. "The cupboards looked beautiful when we finished."

There was one night in particular my mom will never forget. "Your dad woke up in the middle of the night, needing to go to the bathroom. I was sound asleep next to him, when all of a sudden his shouting woke me up. Because I had moved the bedroom furniture around that day, he was disoriented and couldn't find the door to the bathroom and banged into the wall. We laughed about that for years but kept a night light on after that," Mom recalled.

Gee, I'm getting a sense of déjà vu here. The same thing happened to Michael one night, only it was a footstool rather than a wall that he banged into.

Since I apprenticed under the master rearranger, I learned my craft well and can move knickknacks—and heavy furniture—with the best of them. But sometimes it drives Michael up the wall. Like when I change the living room

135

three times in four months. He just doesn't see the need for rearranging things. As far as he's concerned, if it ain't broke, don't fix it.

My husband's into utilitarian. And precise. This is a man who pulls out his tape measure at a moment's provocation, even to hang pictures on the wall.

I'm more of an eyeball-it, guesstimate, jump-right-in kind of gal myself. Which is why we have seven nail holes for one picture. But hey, that's why they invented spackle. IMPORTANT HOUSEHOLD TIP: If you run out of spackle, use toothpaste—just not the blue gel kind.

> **IMPORTANT HOUSEHOLD TIP: If you run out of spackle, use toothpaste—just not the blue gel kind.**

I'm also into pretty. Pretty is essential. So are angles.

When I'm sitting in the living room at night reading or watching a movie, my eyes will sometimes focus in on something that doesn't look quite right. So I'll jump up and angle a teacup or a china plate on the hutch to display it to better advantage. Only now the rest of the shelf is out of whack. So now I need to move a couple of my miniature English cottages to fill in the space. Before I know it, I'm rearranging the entire hutch—which doesn't bother Michael because it doesn't involve him. It's when I say, "You know, I think the couch would look better on that wall" that he groans.

Because it's never just the couch. If we move the couch, we have to move the loveseat too. And if we move the loveseat, we have to move the coffee table. And wouldn't it look nicer if the walls were whipped-butter yellow rather than eggshell? And on and on, ad infinitum.

Can you say snowball effect?

Michael says it's more like an avalanche.

But I don't really see that. Of course, that's because I'm usually too busy roaring through anyone or anything that gets in my decorating path.

Our friends Pat and Ken have been married for thirty-five years and learned early on not to rearrange together. Once during the first year of their marriage, Ken was trying to center a picture on the wall, so he asked his eyeballing bride, "How's this, dear?"

"You need to move it half an inch to the right," his sweetheart answered.

Ken willingly complied.

"No, that's not quite right. Now you need to move it a little to the left, say half an inch or so," Pat said.

Ken complied.

"No, that's not quite right. Try maybe a quarter inch to the right instead."

That was the end of their picture-hanging pas de deux. Now Ken relies on his trusty tape measure rather than his wife.

Must be a male thing. As I mentioned earlier, Michael's a measuring guy too, while I'm the eyeball-it queen. It may take me several tries and multiple nail holes to get it right, but my pictures always wind up centered and straight. I just have to refrain from jumping up and straightening family and friends' crooked pictures when I visit.

But a few friends have specifically asked for my decorating help and rearranging advice—which I'm very definite about. No problem making a decision here. See, don't you think I'd be perfect on one of those decorating shows? Then I could adjust and rearrange to my heart's content. And get paid for it in the process.

You can bet there's no way I'd ever let some stranger have carte blanche in *my* house though. Touch my teacups and die.

---

*The wise woman builds her house, but with her own hands the foolish one tears hers down.*

—PROVERBS 14:1

# 13

## it's a small world (or, the joys of cottage life)

•••

*Although Thomas Kinkade would probably roll over in his paint if he saw my 350-year-old Pepto-Bismol-pink English cottage.*

Sometimes less really is more.

I know there's a tendency these days to go all out with the *bigger is better* approach when remodeling or building homes.

But not always.

Although I'm the first to admit that I'd love a bigger bathroom where I could sink deep into a claw foot tub or sprawl out in one of those larger models with Jacuzzi jets *and* have a separate shower—and I would *kill* for just one walk-in closet!—there's something to be said about the sweet warmth and coziness of a smaller home. Like a bungalow or, better yet, a cottage.

My love affair with cottages began nearly twenty-five years ago when I lived in a small village in England in a centuries-old cottage. As much as the British tire of hearing our American descriptions of "quaint" and "charming," that's exactly what my little Chapel Yard cottage was.

Both quaint *and* charming.

Chapel Yard. The name itself evokes a feeling of peace and serenity. The 350-year-old stone cottage was so named because it stands next door to the local chapel in a small village town in the county of Oxfordshire. And I had the wonderful privilege of living there for nine months when I was stationed in England.

I can still recall my first sight of the cottage—set back from the road and completely invisible to passers-by due to the thick abundance of trees and shrubbery that surrounded it. My roommate and I made our way over an uneven stone walk past the centuries-old small chapel to an antique wrought-iron gate, which bore the inscription "Chapel Yard" etched on a wood plaque.

The gate creaked on its hinges as we passed through it with our prospective landlord. But I scarcely noticed, as I was transfixed by the picture-postcard sight of the little cottage before me.

It was a lovely old stone cottage (*charming* was the word most Americans applied to it, the landlord informed us) complete with lattice-work leaded-glass windows, a small, white wooden door, and wooden shutters. The only discordant note in the whole fairytale-like setting was the color.

Pink. Not a soft, pale hue or even a gentle dusty rose but bordering more on a Pepto-Bismol pink.

Once inside the cottage, however, we quickly forgot the color—I keep wanting to spell it colour in homage to its English locale—as we made our way through the dark tiled foyer into the sitting room at the front of the house. I gasped in delight as my eyes took in the low-beamed ceiling and ancient hardwood floor. The latter was partially covered by a dusty-rose carpet (no Pepto-Bismol pink *this* time), upon which reposed a rose-floral chintz loveseat and chair. The window curtains were of the same flowered chintz fabric, as was the covering on the small, many-paned garden door.

**Pink. Not a soft, pale hue or even a gentle dusty rose but bordering more on a Pepto-Bismol pink.**

We walked through the room slowly, oohing and aahing over all the intricate details, and as we turned around to face the front of the room, I knew I was in heaven. There, in all its old-world glory, stood a centuries-old fireplace complete with mantel. And as if that weren't enough, next to it was a built-in floor-to-ceiling bookcase and beside that a window seat where I could curl up with a "cuppa" and my Agatha Christie. I'd found my cottage haven and was quite prepared to sign the lease then and there, but my ever-so-practical roommate reminded me that we still needed to see the rest of the cottage.

In a romantic haze, I followed the two of them through a large, surprisingly modern kitchen, a small yet adequate bathroom, and then back through the foyer again as we climbed the narrow stairs to the bedrooms.

At the top of the stairs was a small window overlooking the surrounding lush countryside. And to the right of that was the master bedroom, which was to be mine because I won the coin toss.

Once again a beamed ceiling and gorgeous wide-planked hardwood floor met my eye. But the charm in this room lay in the bed. (No pun intended.) It was set in a small alcove in a world all its own, and as I lay within its safe hemisphere and gazed upward, I could well imagine how Heidi must have felt.

I'd found my home.

My roommate Diane and I loved our little Chapel Yard cottage and spent nine blissful months living there. We got to know our neighbor across the street, "old Tom," and were regulars at the neighborhood pub, the Gardiner Arms, which stood just kitty-corner from our house. We'd go there often and have melted-cheese-and-mushroom baps (hot sandwiches on a special floury roll) always followed by a to-die-for chocolate cake topped with marzipan icing and drenched in thick English cream.

The memory of that cake was still with me when I returned to the pub and my old village twenty-one years later to show my beloved where I once lived. I tried to order both a bap and the cake, but the young waiter, who hadn't even been born yet when Diane and I used to frequent the pub, gave me a strange look and said the pub had changed ownership at least three times in the past two decades, as had the menu.

Guess you really can't go home again, or at least not to the pub again. Never mind. I ordered a melted-cheese-and-mushroom sandwich on a baguette, and Michael had a ploughman's lunch (thick, crusty bread and a chunk of cheese). Yum.

We visited the pub and my old cottage on September 12, 2001, the day after the terrible terrorist attacks on the United States.

Michael and I were still shell-shocked and grief stricken, having just heard the news the night before—halfway through our tenth anniversary trip, which also happened to be Michael's first time to the UK. Dazed and bereft, as much as I loved my beloved England, that day all I wanted was to be home.

And Chapel Yard, where I'd once lived two decades before, was the closest thing to it.

As we approached the iron gate, my homesick fingers reached out to trace the old familiar lettering on the now-smooth wood plaque. I hesitated pushing open the gate, not wanting to be a rude American and intrude on the owner's privacy, but Michael, my California-casual husband, encouraged me onward.

We knocked on the front door and, when no one answered, turned to leave after stealing a quick peek through the window that sported what looked like the same floral chintz curtains from twenty-one years before.

But suddenly a movement inside caught my eye, and I glimpsed a white-haired woman making her way toward us.

The tall, casually clad seventy-something Englishwoman opened the door with a quizzical look on her face. Red-faced, I rushed to explain. "Hi, I hate to disturb you, but we're visiting from the States, and twenty-odd years ago I lived here with my roommate, Diane, when we were both stationed at RAF Upper Heyford—"

"Laura?" she said.

Oh my goodness! It was my former landlady, and she still remembered me after all these years—even though we'd only rented out the cottage for a mere nine months.

"How lovely to see you," she said. "It's just lucky you caught me here. My daughter and her family are abroad on holiday, and I'm just stopping by to bring in their post and water the garden. A few more minutes and I'd have been gone."

I love God's timing. He always brings us what we need—at the very moment we need it the most.

"Would you like to come in for a moment?" she asked.

*Would I?*

A wave of nostalgia hit me full force as I walked across the threshold of the faded but still familiar little pink cottage.

Only it wasn't quite so little anymore.

The front sitting room, which did in fact still bear the same floral chintz curtains as when I'd lived there more than twenty years earlier, was now the formal dining room, and I was delighted to spot an antique Blue Willow platter—the same everyday china we use at home—on one of the built-in bookcases.

And the kitchen looked exactly the same, even down to the very same table and high-backed cane chairs I remembered. The only difference was the walls had been painted a bright yellow.

As we left the kitchen, our kind Chapel Yard guide pointed to a closed door at one end of the foyer and said, "And this is . . ."

"I know," I interrupted with a pleased smile as I grabbed the handle and pulled the door open with a wide flourish, "the bathroom."

Except there was no longer a tub or toilet. Instead, the place I used to take long, relaxing Radox baths on cold winter nights had been converted into a small boy's bedroom.

So much for not being a rude American.

But my former landlady was all graciousness as she said, "They've made a few changes over the years," and proceeded to kindly show us the rest of the house. Her daughter and son-in-law had extended the cottage to add on a larger sitting room, two baths, and a couple extra bedrooms to meet the needs of their growing family. The addition was so seamless that it didn't change the cozy cottage charm I loved and remembered so well.

And I felt safe and secure within its snug walls.

I'll always be grateful that during such a frightening, devastating time when we were across the ocean so far away from home, God returned me to my former home—a much-needed haven of peace and tranquility.

*Reflect upon your present blessings—of which every man has many—not on your past misfortunes, of which all men have some.*

—CHARLES DICKENS

# 14

## who needs a marriage counselor? just hire a contractor

...

*There comes a time in every do-it-yourself couple's life when it becomes necessary to lay down the hammer and cough up the dough—especially if you want to save your marriage.*

Scripture says that two are better than one because they have a good return for their labor (Eccles. 4:9).

Not to contradict the Bible, but I think that applies to just about everything in marriage *except* do-it-yourself remodeling and renovation projects. During those home-improvement times, marriage is like going through labor, even for childless couples. As a pastor friend's neighbor always says, "A man's home is his hassle."

Take our friend Carl, who thought it would be grand fun to renovate a house on an acre out in the country and later sell it. His wife, Jan, showed up thinking she would pick out wallpaper and paint kitchen knobs. "My first job was helping him dig a trench ('I only need you for a few minutes,' he said) so he could lay a French drain," Jan recalled.

"Why?" she asked.

"Because there's water pooling up on the side of the house."

"Who cares? Nobody goes out there. Plant water lilies," she replied.

"Carl had me out there in the heat of summer jamming PVC pipe pieces together in a narrow ditch," Jan said. "I always like to make a game out of the work he ropes me into, but there is no way to amuse yourself when you are sniffing glue in a dirty furrow."

"What's the matter, honey?" Carl asked his crimson-faced, sweat-browed wife. "You're not usually this quiet."

Jan snarled.

This gives new meaning to the term *trench warfare*.

My friend offers these renovation words of wisdom to other couples. "It's always a bigger project than we thought. Seems it always costs more and takes twice as long. Now whenever we dream of a project, I always estimate one-third more than we think we'll spend. Then I'm not in shock when the Visa bill comes."

> **"It's always a bigger project than we thought," Jan said. "Seems it always costs more and takes twice as long."**

Ken, the consummate do-it-yourselfer, will often need his wife Pat's help for just a few minutes to hand him something while he's on a ladder. "It never fails," Ken said. "I'll be standing there with a drill between my knees, screws in my mouth, one hand holding up a piece of tile or crown molding, and I stick out my other free hand for her to give me the piece I need, and she's completely oblivious, not paying attention, and looking all around."

Ken can't open his mouth to speak or the screws he needs will fall out, and he can't move from his precarious position or *he'll* fall. So he's reduced to making a kind of grunting noise to get his wife's attention.

"Well, it gets boring just standing there," Pat said in her defense. She added that Ken's whole personality changes when he does a project.

"I'm very focused," Ken said. "She is not."

For instance, a couple years ago they needed to replace an oven in their kitchen. Ken knew it was going to be tricky because it was a tight fit to get the heavy oven into the exact wall cutout—it had to be lifted perfectly straight up and in. If the oven was tilted even the slightest bit, it wouldn't work.

Ken enlisted the aid of his grown son Shane one Saturday.

"Can I help?" his not-so-handy wife asked.

"No. Please do *not* help," Ken said, asking Pat to go stand out of the way while he and Shane accomplished the difficult maneuver.

Father and son lifted the more than 150-pound oven up to the cutout, but it wouldn't fit. Ken couldn't understand. He *knew* it would fit—he'd measured perfectly. What he didn't know, and couldn't see initially, was that Pat, seeing what a hard, heavy job it was, had scooted over to help her husband and son and was pushing from below—at an angle.

In the process, the heavy oven cut Ken's hand—or rather, "shredded" it, as he recalls.

Not the best marital moment.

But although Pat may not be much help in the heavy-lifting department, she makes up for it in other ways. When Ken is working on a project, especially outside in the heat, she'll go out and put cold compresses on his neck and head and make sure her honey is hydrated by bringing him water and also snacks when he gets hungry.

"She takes very good care of me," Ken said.

"Yep," his wife agreed, casting him a loving smile. "Just don't ask me to help."

Although my friends Lisa and Hank nearly killed each other a few times during their home-improvement efforts, they also had fun.

"Hank fell through the ceiling while trying to put up a fan," Lisa said. "And another time when he checked the hot wires in the attic, they were dead, so he came down to work."

Then my friend heard a short-circuit sound, and her husband was quiet. "Needless to say, he was a bit frazzled," Lisa recalled, "and said, 'Oops, that one was hot.' He worries me sometimes."

Another time, Hank was attempting to adhere the fireplace mantel to the wall using a standard tile setting adhesive. Two weeks later, while he was hanging a five-hundred-pound piece of angel wall art, the mantel fell off. He learned that instead of tile adhesive, he should have used epoxy.

The couple says they have learned a few rules about remodeling together:

Compromise.
Let her have her way, or you will pay.
If all else fails, consult the manual.
Paint fights can be fun.

> **Compromise.
> Let her have her way,
> or you will pay.
> If all else fails,
> consult the manual.
> Paint fights
> can be fun.**

Cousin Debbie, who's been married to Roy for more than two decades, has learned an important lesson about working with her husband on household projects over the years—one that creates a harmonious atmosphere in the home: "He has the final say," she said dryly.

Another cousin, Barb, has learned over the years to adopt the same strategy. "There's only one way of doing things—his way. To deal with it, I just say, 'Yes sir, no sir,' and do whatever he wants, or I try to find reasons to escape. It's easier to go along than to start a war. It usually ends up looking nice anyway."

My friend Andrea is the queen of changing her mind—and focus. And nowhere was this more evident than when she and Bill were remodeling their fixer-upper home. One week she'd want front yard sprinklers installed. Then it would be, "Let's finish the basement in a shabby chic style complete with chandeliers." The next week it would be, "Let's cover the basement walls with brick, and we'll do galvanized lighting." Or "How about installing a Murphy bed so your mother can sleep in the basement when she visits?"

To date, Bill has built and installed the Murphy bed, just in time for his mother's latest visit. "She came, she slept, she left. It was a lovely visit," Andrea said. Since then Andrea's been online searching for the perfect shabby chic chandelier while Bill finished installing the sprinklers—on his birthday.

Andrea became—how can I say this?—*more* than obsessed with the house remodel. Once she got up at 1:30 a.m. and turned the floodlights on in the backyard to do a little rose pruning. "I was resketching the placement of the pond and fountain for the umpteenth time when Bill woke up and yelled, 'Get back to bed, Edward Scissorhands. You're out of your mind! You need a therapist.'"

Andrea admits that she got really caught up in everything being "absolutely perfect."

Bill, who is incredibly handy around the house and who I think invented the term *hard worker* did almost all the remodeling single-handedly.

And it began to take its toll.

After four years of nonstop work—in addition to his full-time teaching job—ripping out and repairing; plastering, plumbing, and painting; and wiring and woodcutting, Bill grew clinically depressed.

"He says it started the week after we moved in," Andrea said, but he just tried to work through it.

Having been medicated for his depression, Bill kept his pills in a plastic container, much like the one the couple kept their dog's medicine in. One day Bill mistakenly took the dog's phenobarbital instead of his Prozac. He called the

151

poison control center, and they said, "If you start barking, you need to come in."

His depression immobilized him to the point where he simply couldn't do any more work.

None. Nada. Zip.

Realizing that her husband's health and their marriage were far more important than any house, no matter how beautiful, the couple seriously considered selling their home. "Bill was so overwhelmed by this point that he *hated* the house, so we almost sold it," Andrea recalled. "But then we thought, *If we sold it, we couldn't sell it as is.*"

Now it was Andrea's turn to grow depressed.

Not a good thing. Husband and wife were both tremendously discouraged and weighed down at the same time and didn't know what to do. So they sought counseling.

Their counselor encouraged them to cash out some of their retirement money and hire a contractor to help with the house. The at-the-end-of-their-rope couple followed her advice, took money out of their retirement fund, and hired a licensed contractor—who happened to be a Christian and let them pay at their own pace. "He would bring us Christian music, pray with us, and give us books," Andrea recalled. "It brought such a confident feeling to have him in our house."

One day when Bill and Andrea arrived home from work, they discovered on the fireplace a piece of wood into which their contractor had whittled the name *Jesus*.

Four years later—and eight years after they bought the house—their lovely home is so gorgeous that it's been featured in the Interiors section of their local paper a couple times.

"Bill's fine now," Andrea reported, "the house is beautiful, and we're done in terms of remodeling."

Although, knowing my style-conscious friend, decorating's another story.

Maria, a former therapist who's now a university professor, said when she looks back on the times when she and her husband were remodeling their 1920s farmhouse, she occasionally wonders how they ever made it through it.

Yet she's also grateful for the growth it provided in their marriage.

"Ralph and I discovered we work very well together," Maria said. "I learned I had a lot more strength than I thought, and he learned that a lot of his surgeon's eye for detail and his craft of working with his hands was transferable. Our home was gorgeous when we left it—and complete."

That must be due to Maria's former profession.

Michael and I didn't fare as well working together on a major renovation project. Of course, part of the problem was that when we finally had the time and the cash to do our long-planned backyard makeover, we picked the hottest July in California history to begin. Temperatures soared over 105 most days, and tempers flared equally hot.

After one particularly frustrating and horrible day when everything went wrong—after weeks and weeks of delays, workers not showing up, unexpected expenses, things breaking, and myriad other things going wrong—Michael finally reached the zenith of his stress level. My husband exploded. "I hate this shed, I hate this yard, I hate this house!"

My helpful reply?

"Well, let's just sell it then. The market's great right now, and we could get double what we paid for the house, pay off all our debts, take a trip to England, and still buy or rent a nice condo where we wouldn't have to worry about yard work or maintenance."

That was one time when I should have put into practice the proverb, "Silence is golden."

My timing may have been lousy, but my motive was sincere.

As much as I love our cute cottagey home and all the work we've put into it—inside and out—I love my husband and our marriage even more. And should the day ever come when we need or choose to sell our home, that would be okay. At the end of the day, it is just a house. And I can make any house a home.

Home is, after all, where the heart is, and my husband is my heart.

Besides, I'm pretty sure that anywhere else we moved wouldn't have that hated harvest-gold linoleum.

---

*This is the true nature of home—it is the place of peace; the shelter, not only from injury, but from all terror, doubt and division.*

---

—JOHN RUSKIN

# acknowledgments

Paint cans of thanks to all those who shared their remodeling and renovation horror stories with me: Lori Birtwell, Judi Braddy, Lisa Brys, Peggy Clark, Barb Colwell, Bob Cullifer, Bill and Andrea Cuthbertson, Joyce Dingman, Lonnie Hull DuPont, Bettie Eichenberg, David Eichenberg, Bettie Fiscus, Shane Galloway, Sharon and Jim Hetland, Maria Hunt, Laurie Kehler, Debbie and Roy Madearis, Deborah McCaffrey, Pat and Ken McLatchey, Kim Orendor, Annette Smith, Jill Vanderbrug, Lana and Michael Yarbrough, Katie Young, Jeannie and Johnny Zapara, with an extra bucketful of thanks to my writer pal Jan Coleman for always going that extra mile. (Just remember to watch where you step, Jan.)

A houseful of thanks to my talented carpenter brother Dave, who happily shared stories from the other side of the construction fence.

Sincere gratitude to Judith Martinez at the Antelope Home Depot, who personifies "customer service."

Once again, grateful thanks to Chip MacGregor, my friend and a prince among agents, who handles all that yucky negotiating and business stuff so I don't have to and continues to champion my writing. (Thanks also to Alice Crider, his right-hand assistant.)

To editor extraordinaire Lonnie Hull DuPont, one of the best in the business: Thank you for always believing in me. I consider it a privilege to work with you. And to call you friend.

To my Baker/Revell family: We did it again, guys! Thanks!

And lastly, heartfelt thanks to my friends and family who support and encourage me as I do what I love. Especially Michael, the sun, moon, and wind beneath my wings. He's also the poor guy who has to put up with my neurotic mood swings when I'm on deadline. There needs to be a special place in heaven for the husbands of writers. With padded walls. (Having said that, can I have my kitchen now, honey? "Shut the door.")

**Laura Jensen Walker** is the author of several humor books, including *Dated Jekyll, Married Hyde*; *Love Handles for the Romantically Impaired*; *Thanks for the Mammogram!*; *Mentalpause*; *Through the Rocky Road and into the Rainbow Sherbet*; and *Girl Time*. A popular speaker and a breast cancer survivor, she knows firsthand the healing power of laughter. She and her husband, Michael, live in Sacramento, California.

For information on having Laura Jensen Walker speak at your event, or to learn more about Laura, please visit her website at www.laurajensenwalker.com. To write Laura, please email her at Laura@laurajensenwalker.com or write to her at P.O. Box 601325, Sacramento, CA 95860.

You are so overdue for some good chick flicks, chatter, and chocolate!

Memory loss, hot flashes, a few extra tears . . . Learn to laugh through these hormonal hassles!

Hope, help, and a little humor for cancer patients, survivors, and caregivers.